The *NEW* Complete
ILLUSTRATION GUIDE

**THE ULTIMATE TRACE FILE
FOR ARCHITECTS,
DESIGNERS, ARTISTS,
AND STUDENTS**

Revised and Enlarged 2nd Edition

by LARRY EVANS

WITH ILLUSTRATIONS BY NANCIE WEST SWANBERG

VAN NOSTRAND REINHOLD
I(T)P® A Division of International Thomson Publishing Inc.

New York • Albany • Bonn • Boston • Detroit • London • Madrid • Melbourne
Mexico City • Paris • San Francisco • Singapore • Tokyo • Toronto

I(T)P® an International Thomson Publishing Company
The ITP logo is a registered trademark used herein under license

Printed in the United States of America

For more information, contact:

Van Nostrand Reinhold
115 Fifth Avenue
New York, NY 10003

Chapman & Hall GmbH
Pappelallee 3
69469 Weinheim
Germany

Chapman & Hall
2-6 Boundary Row
London
SE1 8HN
United Kingdom

International Thomson Publishing Asia
221 Henderson Road #05-10
Henderson Building
Singapore 0315

Thomas Nelson Australia
Japan
102 Dodds Street
South Melbourne, 3205
Victoria, Australia

International Thomson Publishing

Hirakawacho Kyowa Building, 3F
2-2-1 Hirakawacho
Chiyoda-ku, 102 Tokyo
Japan

Nelson Canada
1120 Birchmount Road
Scarborough, Ontario
Canada M1K 5G4

International Thomson Editores
Seneca 53
Col. Polanco
11560 Mexico D.F. Mexico

2 3 4 5 6 7 8 9 10   QEB-KP   02 01 00 99 98 97

Library of Congress Cataloging-in-Publication Data

Evans, Larry, 1939-
    The new complete illustration guide : the ultimate trace file for
architects, designers, artists, and students / by Larry Evans ; with
illustrations by Nancie West Swanberg.
        p.   cm.
    Updated ed. of: Complete illustration guide for architects,
designers, artists, and students.
    ISBN 0-442-02239-5
    1. Architectural rendering--Technique.   I. Swanberg, Nancie.
II. Evans, Larry, 1939-   Complete illustration guide for architects,
designers, artists, and students. III. Title.
NA2780.E9   1996
720'.28'4--dc20
                                                    96-21519
                                                    CIP

CONTENTS

The Hotel Netherland - New York City, circa 1890

INTRODUCTION

When I was growing up, I often wondered about my older relatives who had been born in the 19th century and had lived from the "Horse and Buggy" days, through the invention of the automobile and airplane, and on to see a man walk on the moon. The huge advances in technology, it seemed to me, were so massive that I assumed no person could adequately cope with them. Well, no advance in technology could rival the invention of the personal computer and the changes this invention has wrought upon the architectural and commercial art world.

When the first Illustration Guide tracing sheets were created in 1964, all the artwork had to be copied by a stat camera, printed to size on photographic paper, cut, and pasted on a layout board for the printer. Type had to be obtained from the typesetter, corrected, reset, and pasted in position. Getting figure and vehicle drawings to scale was a giant task. In those days we created rubber stamps to help make the job of producing repetitive images go a little faster. Nothing much changed in the production of the tracing sheets through the 1970s. Those years saw huge world-wide sales of rubber stamps of plan trees, vehicles, and figures. Transfer sheets of these images were produced and sold everywhere. By 1982, when the first edition of *Illustration Guide For Architects, Designers, Artists, and Students* was published, all the pages had to be prepared as described above.

Then around 1983, I purchased my first Mac. It was so tiny (128 bytes of RAM) that the only thing it could do was run out of memory. But it was a major breakthrough. You could almost set type on it. The upgrade to a 512 was earthshaking. Then a Mac Plus, containing an entire Meg of internal RAM...well you know the story. There appears to be no end to the upgrades. Computers now control the graphic arts industry (including architecture). The rubber stamps have been sent to the museum to be exhibited along with Egyptian scarabs (also used as rubber stamps in 3000 BC). These pages are all created on a computer more powerful than the one used to send that guy mentioned earlier to the moon. By the time you read this, *that* computer will be obsolete.

With artwork now digitalized, a new era of rubber stamp images has evolved. During production of the latest update of this book, the programs used to draw the images were also updated. Whole new options were opened, especially in the color section. Some selected material is available on the Internet at http://www.vnr.com/vnr/evans/evans.html as the whole purpose of this book is to help architects and other professionals create illustrations more easily.

The NEW Complete Illustration Guide has been created for use in the drafting rooms and design studios of architects and artists. It is a book for you to use, a tool, much like a T-square, to trace, cut-up, copy, and learn from. If you have any suggestions for material you would like to see included in future editions of this journal, please let the publisher hear about them.

HOW TO USE THIS BOOK

The secret formula for creating good renderings is very simple: build a strong perspective drawing. There exist today several acceptable methods for the formulation of a perspective:

1. The two elevation system
2. The top plan system
3. The measuring point system
4. The cube system

Each has its champions, so it's up to you to decide just which method suits your purpose. After 20 years of professional renderings, I have found that the "cube" method best serves my need for quick, accurate layouts.

Building the Perspective

1. Selection of view

Most renderings are structured from plans and elevations. These drawings are usually in scale, so horizontal and vertical measurements are marked on the drawing.

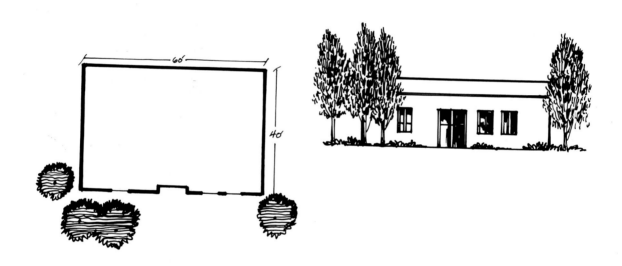

Using a 30° – 60° triangle, select your proposed station point on the plan.

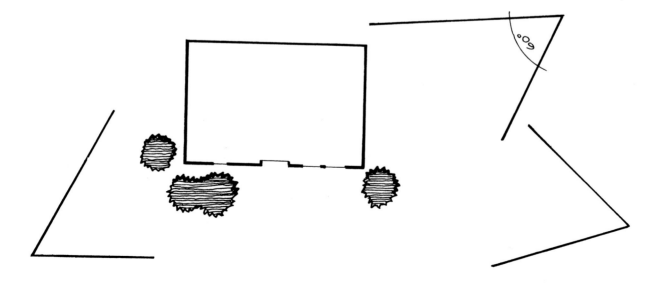

Make quick freehand studies of each proposed view.

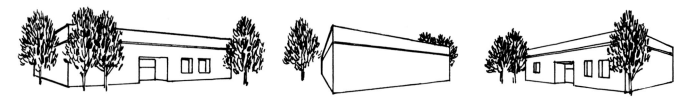

At this stage in the development of your perspective, you must choose your eye level and the distance you wish to be from the building (station point).

2. The full size block-out

At this point you are satisfied with the view and the eye level has been established. Projecting the quick study up to finished drawing size requires a few momentous decisions:

    A. Selection of the size of the finished drawing (let's try 24″ x 36″)

    B. Selection of the size of the building within the borders

    C. Creation of a pleasing composition

It should be noted here that the sample building we are using is quite simple and that your project is probably more complicated. The fact is, the "cube" method makes the degree of complication irrelevant. Whatever you need to draw, be it our simple box building or the Eiffel Tower, can be easily constructed using this perspective method.

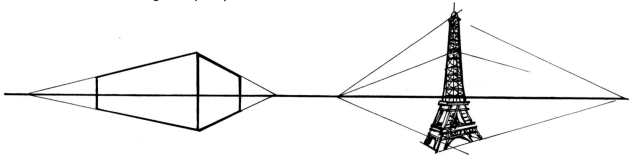

If you feel more confident with the plan projection method of perspective, just remember, as you're setting up your projection system, the rest of us have already begun to draw details in *our* building.

Anyhow . . .

The use of this book as a guide does not require the selection of any particular perspective method, just an *understanding* of whatever method you choose.

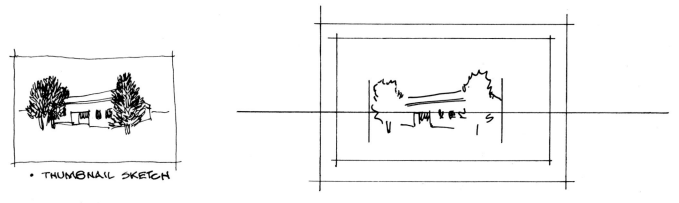

• THUMBNAIL SKETCH

Using your "thumbnail" sketch as a guide, plan the picture composition on the full size sheet.

Selection of Vanishing Points and a Vertical Scale

Your quick thumbnail sketch has in fact established the station point (the spot the viewer of this particular perspective has chosen, i.e., the position of the eye). In the sample drawing, the station point is located on the plan as shown.

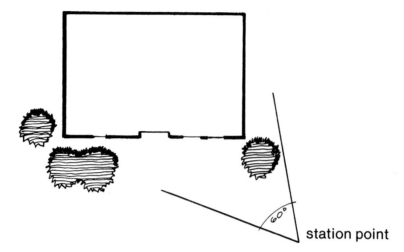

station point

We have decided to view more of the south elevation than the east so our left-hand vanishing point (vp) will be somewhere off the paper.

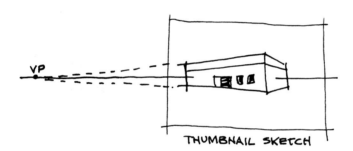

THUMBNAIL SKETCH

But, you say, "How can I locate my vanishing point so far off the paper? My drawing board is only just slightly larger than my paper". Using a T square, build a simple arc system to locate that elusive off-the-board vanishing point.

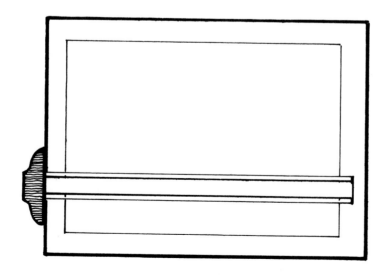

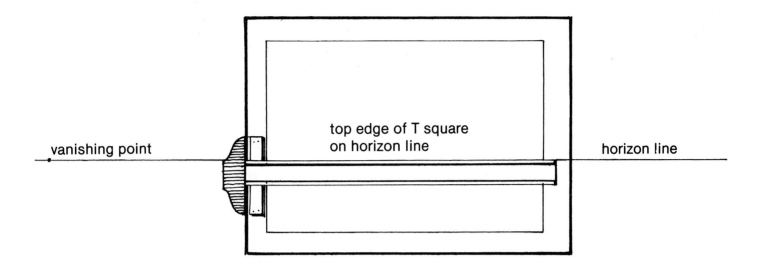

vanishing point   top edge of T square
on horizon line   horizon line

Attach a section of heavy mat board *exactly* the length of the head of your T square to the drawing board (but off the surface of the paper). This piece of mat board is the first section of an arc that will locate the left vanishing point.

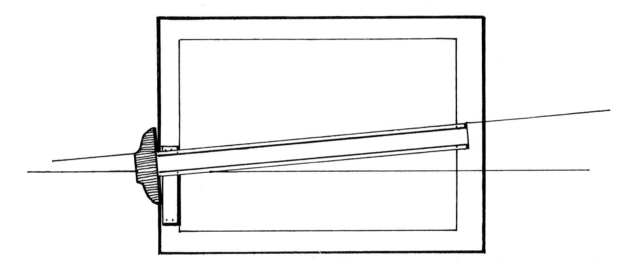

Resting your T square on the mat board strip, draw an angle that closely duplicates the perspective angle you selected on your thumbnail sketch.

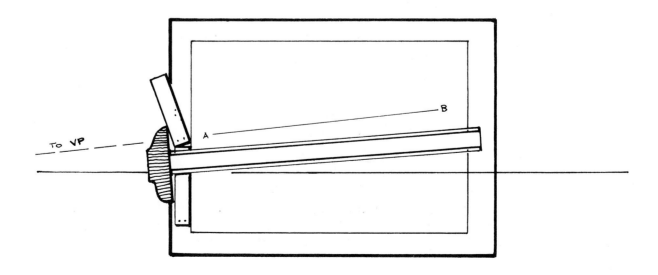

Connect Point *A* to Point *B* and secure a piece of mat board exactly the size of the first section to your drawing board. This arc will give you all of your vanishing lines *above* the horizon. Duplicate the procedure for the bottom vanishing lines and you have found your impossible left vanishing point.

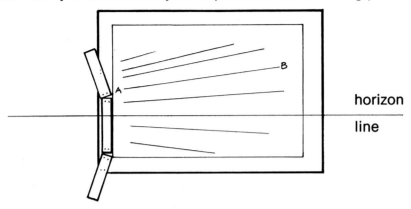

The Vertical Measuring Line
    Let's review what we have done so far:
        A. We have selected a viewing angle and eye level (the thumbnail sketch).
        B. We have located the horizon line on the full size paper and found the left-hand vanishing point.
        C. We have estimated the size the building should be in relation to the rest of the picture.
Now we must locate the vertical measuring line and the right-hand vanishing point.

We know from the thumbnail sketch that we wish to see more of the south face of the building. This means that the leading edge of the building will be somewhere to the right of center on our drawing.

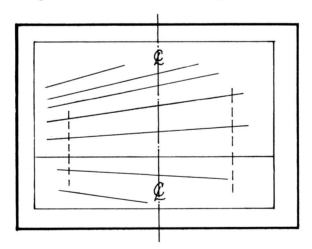

It also means that the right-hand vanishing point will be closer to the center than the left vanishing point.

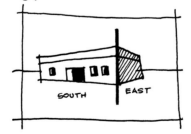

Choose the percentage of south and east faces (back to the thumbnail) and draw the nearest vertical edge of the building on your paper. This vertical is usually used as the vertical measuring line.

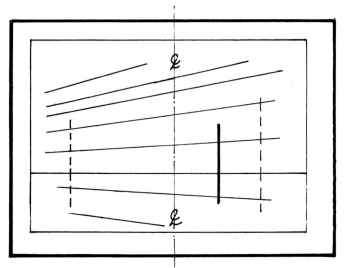

We know from the plans that the building is 22′ tall and that the south face is 60′ long. By measuring the distance from the vertical height line to the left-hand limits of the building area we can develop a scale that will allow the building to fit within our prescribed borders.

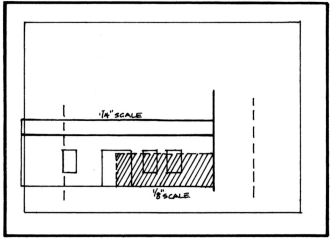

We know that the perspective will diminish the horizontal measurement, so it is just possible that the ¼″ scale might fit our need. Let's try it. First select an eye level at 5′6″ and plot that on the vertical. This gives us the base of the building and a way to locate figures within the picture.

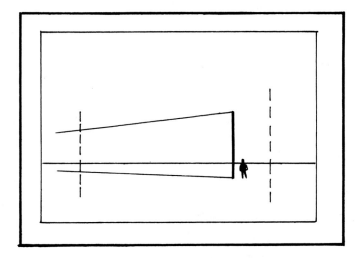

Now let's select the right-hand vanishing point. We know it must fall outside the right-hand edge of the building, and for the sake of sanity, lie within the confines of the drawing board. (One constructed arc per drawing should be enough for anyone.) Let's place it 3″ from the right edge of the building limit.

By connecting the top and bottom points to the right-hand vanishing point, we have established our building in perspective.

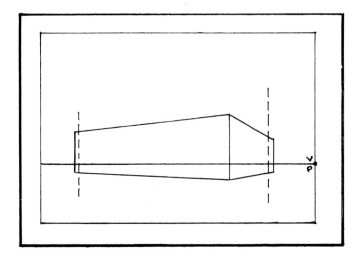

Creating the Measuring Cube within the Perspective

Using the ¼ ″ = 1′ scale we have chosen, mark off 22′ on the vertical height line beginning 5′6″ (in scale) below the horizon line.

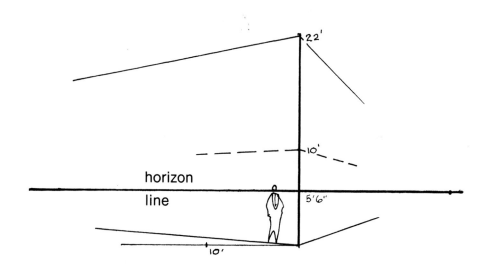

Measure 10′ on the vertical height line and 10′ on a line parallel to the horizon line beginning at the base of the vertical height line. We know that measurements diminish in perspective, so the line indicating the base of the building will be shorter than the horizontal measuring line. This measurement is subjective at best, but when you create the measuring cube within the perspective and it *looks* like a cube, then for all intents and purposes, your perspective measuring system will be close enough.

To find the short side of your cube, draw a diagonal from Point *A*, parallel to the horizon line, that bisects line B/C.

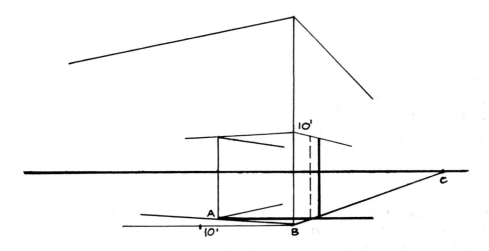

This diagonal will give you a good indication of where the back edge of your cube should be. If your cube is close to the right vanishing point (as in the illustration), the diagonal will give you an edge too close to the vertical height line to look visually correct. Adjust the perspective slightly to create a visually pleasing cube and your measuring cube will be completed.

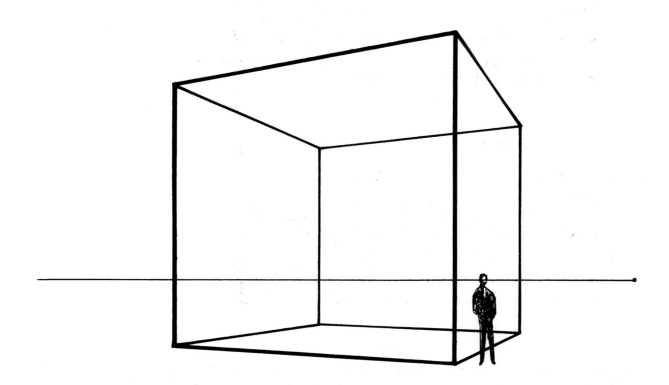

Placing Figures, Trees and Vehicles in the Drawing

Now that your perspective has been constructed, the entourage can easily be inserted into the picture area.

1. Locate the major trees and choose the proper variety.

2. Scan Section III to select the right tree illustration. Trace the tree into your composition. If the size illustrated does not fit correctly, either draw the tree freehand using the illustration as a guide, or have the drawing expanded or reduced by photographic process.

3. Repeat the process for figures, only this time when you place the figures into your picture, use the horizon line to locate them.

4. Vehicles are slightly harder to locate since adjustments must be made to fit them into *your* particular perspective. Use the horizon line to place the vehicles in the proper relationship to the rest of the elements in the drawing.

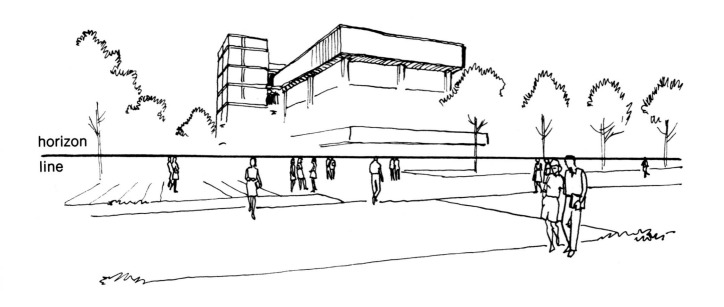

horizon
line

horizon line

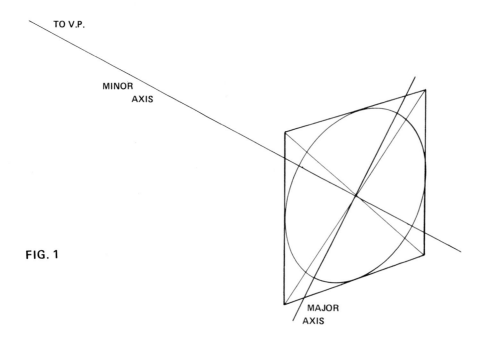

TO V.P.

MINOR
AXIS

FIG. 1

MAJOR
AXIS

CIRCLES & ELLIPSES

With the advent of modern technology, circular buildings are easier to build but are still just as hard to draw as ever. These pages illustrate three important facts about circles in perspective.

Figure 1 shows the circle in perspective (ellipse) in a square also in perspective. The minor axis bisects the center of the ellipse and connects with the left vanishing point. It is called the minor axis because it crosses the ellipse at its narrowest dimension. The major axis connects the farthest dimension of the ellipse.

Figure 2 applies the illustration in Figure 1 to architectural drawing. Notice how the ellipse recedes in degrees as it recedes in perspective.

The two renderings illustrate that the major axis is always parallel to the horizon line when viewed from above or below.

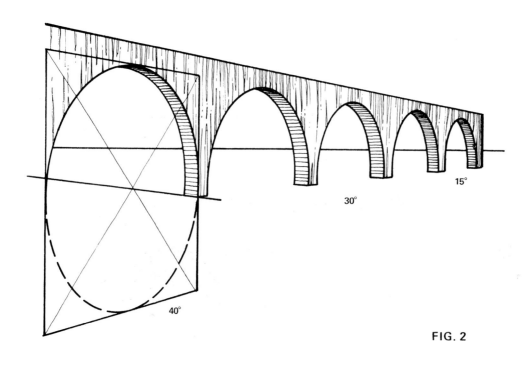

15°

30°

40°

FIG. 2

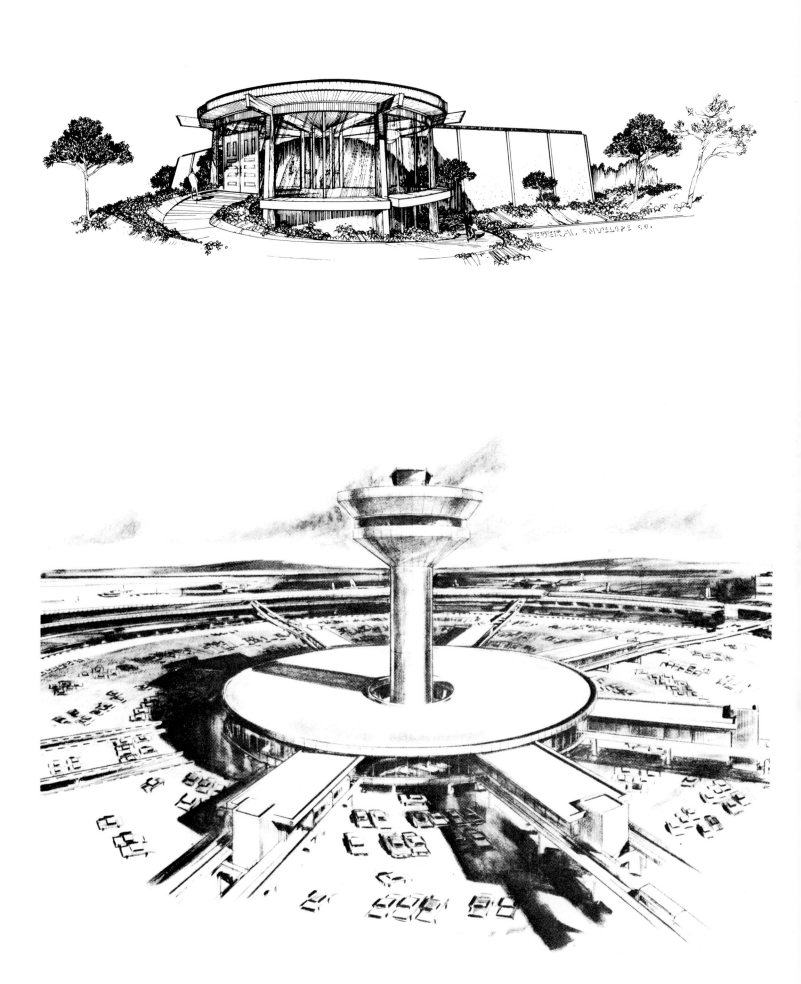

Figure 1

WATERCOLOR RENDERING

One of the most useful tools in the preparation of architectural renderings is the medium of watercolor. Available in tubes from Winsor Newton or Grumbacher and applied with a soft sable brush, watercolor rendering is fast and offers a wide range of textures and colors.

A minimum range of colors is suggested for architectural work. A typical palette is shown in Figure 3.

Figure 1 shows the degree of completion the pencil drawing should be in before the application of color. Remember, watercolor is a transparent medium so lines will show through. Make sure you have the shadows roughed in and the direction of sunlight secured before you proceed with the painting.

Figure 2

Figure 2 illustrates the first wash to apply to the rendering. First tape the edges of the building with Magic Mending or drafting tape. Don't use masking tape as it will pull the paper surface. I use a watercolor board with the paper already mounted on it. If you don't use a board you must make a "stretch" or your paper will buckle and large washes will be impossible to accomplish. Use a handmade 300 lb. paper and you won't have to worry about buckling.

To apply a large wash, such as the sky, wet the entire area (except for the areas you want to leave white) with a large sable brush. Mix the desired color in a cup and "drop in" the color without touching the paper with the brush. Pour the excess off by tilting the board. Be sure to pour off the top and don't get any on the building.

Figure 3

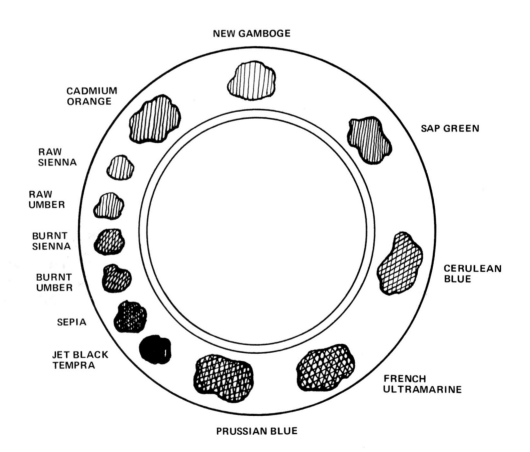

NEW GAMBOGE

CADMIUM
ORANGE

SAP GREEN

RAW
SIENNA

RAW
UMBER

BURNT
SIENNA

CERULEAN
BLUE

BURNT
UMBER

SEPIA

JET BLACK
TEMPRA

FRENCH
ULTRAMARINE

PRUSSIAN BLUE

Figure 4

After the sky dries, begin to render the building (Figure 3). Notice gradations from dark to light in the shadow areas. Try to accomplish the desired tone in one wash. The less over painting you have to do the faster and cleaner your painting will be.

Figure 4 is the finished rendering. Details are completed and rough edges are cleaned up with opaque white. You can mix your watercolors with opaque white to touch up little problem areas.

On the first few renderings you do, it is helpful to prepare a "rough" before actually attempting the final painting. Plan your shadows and composition carefully before doing the finished work.

Figure 1

Figure 2

GLASS

The three illustrations on these pages indicate the basic approach to glass indication. Figure 1 is a watercolor sketch showing a standard double-hung window with drapes. The shadow area on the glass is lighter than the sun-lit area and the darker areas of glass give just a hint of the room beyond. Glass is a lot more reflective in shadow, so use your own judgment. Remember, the final result is what counts. Figures 2 and 3 indicate a "sketchy" approach to rendering that can often create a mood that is lost in more finished renderings.

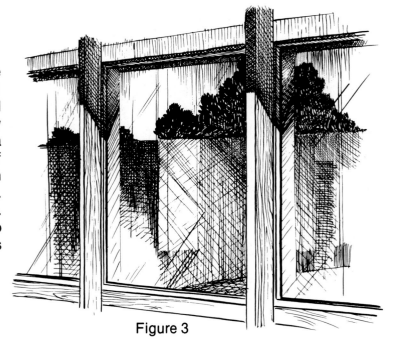

Figure 3

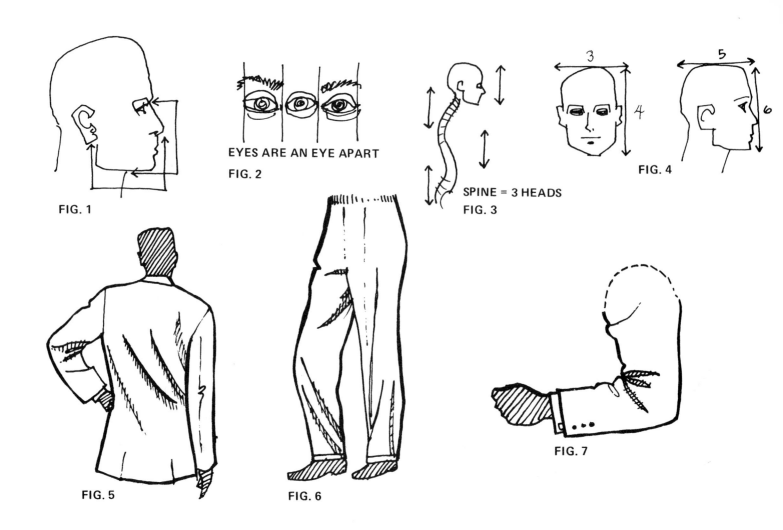

FIG. 1

EYES ARE AN EYE APART
FIG. 2

SPINE = 3 HEADS
FIG. 3

FIG. 4

FIG. 5

FIG. 6

FIG. 7

When drawing the figure, even if you stylize or just block in shapes for scale, proportion and attitude are important features to draw properly if your rendering is to achieve success. The viewer identifies with the people in your drawing and it is not all that difficult to draw people properly.

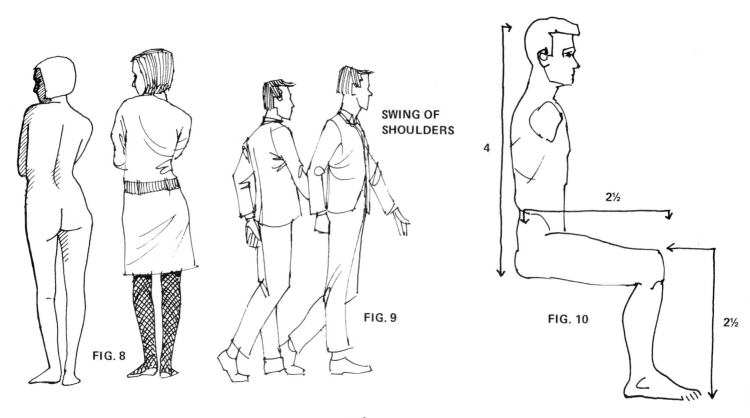

FIG. 8

FIG. 9

SWING OF SHOULDERS

FIG. 10

DRAWING PEOPLE

These pages contain several illustrations showing basic proportions and attitudes. As figures are an important aspect of architectural rendering, the knowledge of proper proportions is equally important.

Figure 1 illustrates that the distance from the eyes to the chin is roughly equal to the distance from the ear to the tip of the nose.

Figure 2 shows spacing between the eyes, and Figure 3 shows that the spine is three heads tall.

Figure 4 draws your attention to the proportion of both front and side views of the head.

Figures 5, 6, & 7 illustrate folds most commonly found in men's suits.

Figure 8 shows a girl standing with her weight on one leg. Notice how the hip on the side that bears the weight pushes upward and out. The leg carrying the weight of the body bends in so that the foot positions itself directly under the head.

Figure 9 shows that when walking, the body turns from side to side, thrusting the shoulders foreward on the opposite side of the body carrying the weight.

Figure 10 illustrates basic proportions of the seated figure.

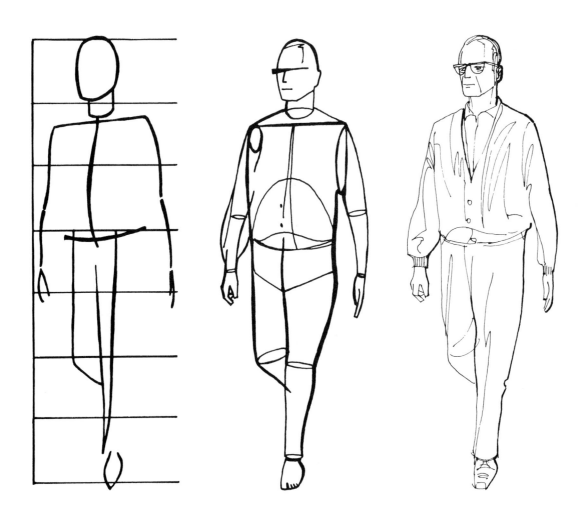

EARLY MASTERS OF RENDERING

The way to apply these renderings to your illustration is to study the line work and composition. Certainly trees and plants are the same today. People are different enough so that modern poses must be used, but the basic drawing is the same. Now that architectural design is swinging back towards ornamentalism, reviewing some of the "old masters" sketches can be usefuf for today's buildings.

EARLY MASTERS

This chapter contains a variety of some of the best illustrations created by past masters of renderings. Of these artists Joseph Pennell was possibly the best and certainly the most prolific.

Joseph Pennell (1860 - 1926) was a magazine illustrator who captured the essence of existing buildings. His ink technique is an excellent example of economy of line. His figures are superb and add a richness of scale and mood to his renderings.

Harry Fenn (1838 -1911) was a prolific artist who specialized in land- scapes and building illustration. He worked mostly in pen and ink but he was also a founder of the American Watercolor Society.

Vestibule of the New York Life building, Minneapolis.

Harry Fenn did the illustrations on these two pages, probably about the size shown here. The perspective of the stairway above is well constructed with the eye level just above the level of the landing.

The drawing on the opposite page makes use of the foreground trees blending into the fabric of the structure but not obscuring it.

Madison Square Garden.

AT VIRE
FRANCE

The use of value patterns in these two illustrations illustrate the basic requirement of preplanning your sketch. The tower above stands dark against a light sky with the toned foreground setting off the light middleground. The skyscraper grouping on the opposite page sets off the light foreground against the darker tower with the shadow from the near wing pushing it forward.

New York skyscrapers circa 1900.

H.M.Pettit

7

8

PROPOSED BUILDING AT SAN FRANCISCO.
WILLIS POLK, ARCHITECT.

THE CHATEAU·MARTAINVILLE
WEST FRONT

The material on the next four pages is taken from a German garden book printed around the turn of the century. The illustration technique is fresh and loose and allows for a good contrast between the foliage and the architecture.

11

Fig. 1.

Fig. 2

Fig. 3.

Fig. 4.

Fig. 12.

Fig. 13.

Fig. 14.

Fig. 15.

ACCESSORIES

Fig. 5.

Fig. 6.

Fig. 7.

Fig. 8.

Fig. 9.

Fig. 10.

Fig. 11.

Fig. 16.

Fig. 17.

Fig. 18.

Fig. 19.

Fig. 20.

Fig. 21.

Fig. 22.

Fig. 23.

Fig. 24.

A turn of the century guide to architectural illustration.

CHATEAV · ST · AGIL
· FRANCE ·

16

RENDERING GALLERY

Ghirardelli Square - San Francisco

RENDERING GALLERY

The illustrations in this chapter are included to show just how the figures, trees, plants and vehicles may be used to enhance an architectural rendering.

The figures in the rendering of San Francisco's famed Ghiradelli Square were copied directly from this book. The trees and plants were drawn to fit the illustration but were patterned after illustrations found in the tree and plant chapters.

Notice how some of the figures overlap each other. This technique helps to create a perception of depth and provides a more realistic view of the actual space.

When inking, a pencil sketch is ALWAYS done first. Notice that the inked drawing below has changed somewhat from the pencil layout. It is almost impossible to make major changes in the ink drawing unless it is done on drafting film. If you ink on film, often after erasing the pen will make a thicker line than before.

24

Architect - Sid Hoover/Robinson, Mills & Williams

The illustration above was done using the preliminary sketch shown on the next two pages. The preliminary drawing is shown at full size. Most illustrations are reproduced at a much smaller size than the original drawing. In order for the lines to hold, the illustrator must carefully choose the proper pen sizes. This drawing was done using a #2 Rapidograph for the street and foliage, a #0 for the buildings and a #00 for the figures. A #000 was used for the brick indication.

The final ink drawing of this project is shown on the preceeding page. The figures were drawn on another sheet to keep the pencil layout less complicated.

28

The trees in this rendering were drawn carefully in pencil before the final inking. They set the mood of the building even though the foreground is really just a parking lot.

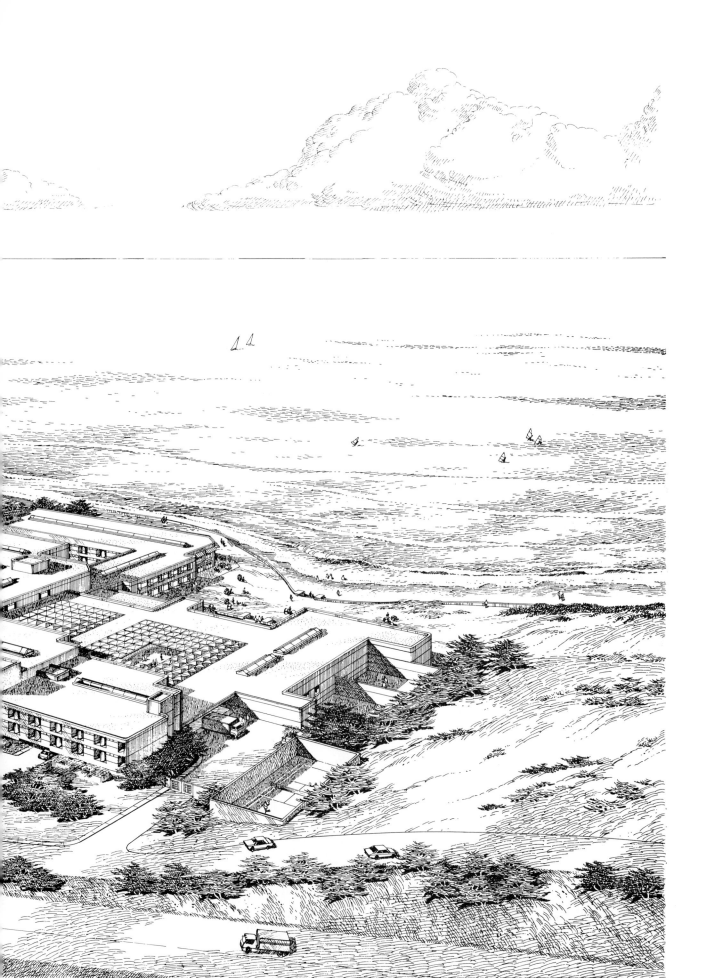

In the rendering of this proposed beachfront hotel, the trunks of the trees have been "tucked under" a bit to help create the illusion of a high viewing angle.

Architect - Robinson, Mills and Williams

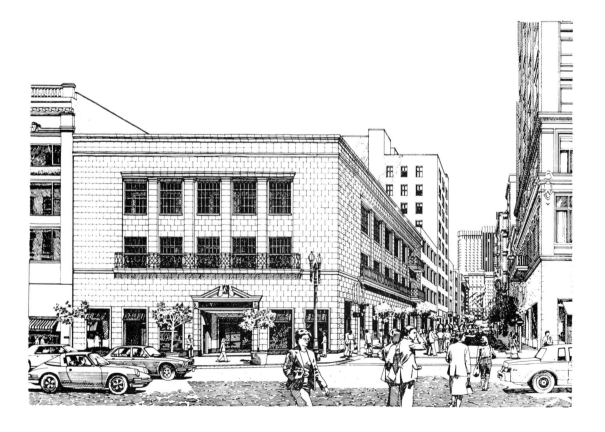

When renderings are made of renovated buildings, special problems are created for the illustrator; integrating existing elements into the new picture when they often are not complementry to the new composition. The renderings on these two pages were done using photographs to establish the view. In each illustration, artistic license was taken to enhance the rendering. For example: The bridge on the opposite page was compiled from three different photos taken from three different station points. The lower illustration on the same page was made up from several different photographs to widen the street and bring the background forward.

Architect - Lomax/Rock Architects/ Johannes Van Tilberg & Partners

Architect - Robinson, Mills and Williams

Architect - Gensler and Associates

Different inking techniques were used on all of these renderings.

THE COLOR SECTION

The next 32 pages contain a new look for the Illustration Guide: *full color illustrations.* Recent advancements in computer graphics have made it possible to create useful illustrations in color. These images are all digitalized and are available through the Internet at http://www.vnr.com/vnr/evans/evans.html. It is the author's wish that the entire contents of this book will be available in computer format soon. If you also share this desire, write to the publisher at the address shown on the copyright page and let your wishes be known.

The illustrations shown here use the figures, trees, and vehicles illustrated in this book. Be careful to position figures and vehicles in their proper relationship to the horizon line. This becomes especially important when figures are in the foreground. The rendering above was first done in pen and ink on mylar. A brownline print was made from the mylar and then colored in marker pen and colored pencil. The rendering below is acrylic on board.

SCALE 1" = 1' & 1/2" = 1'

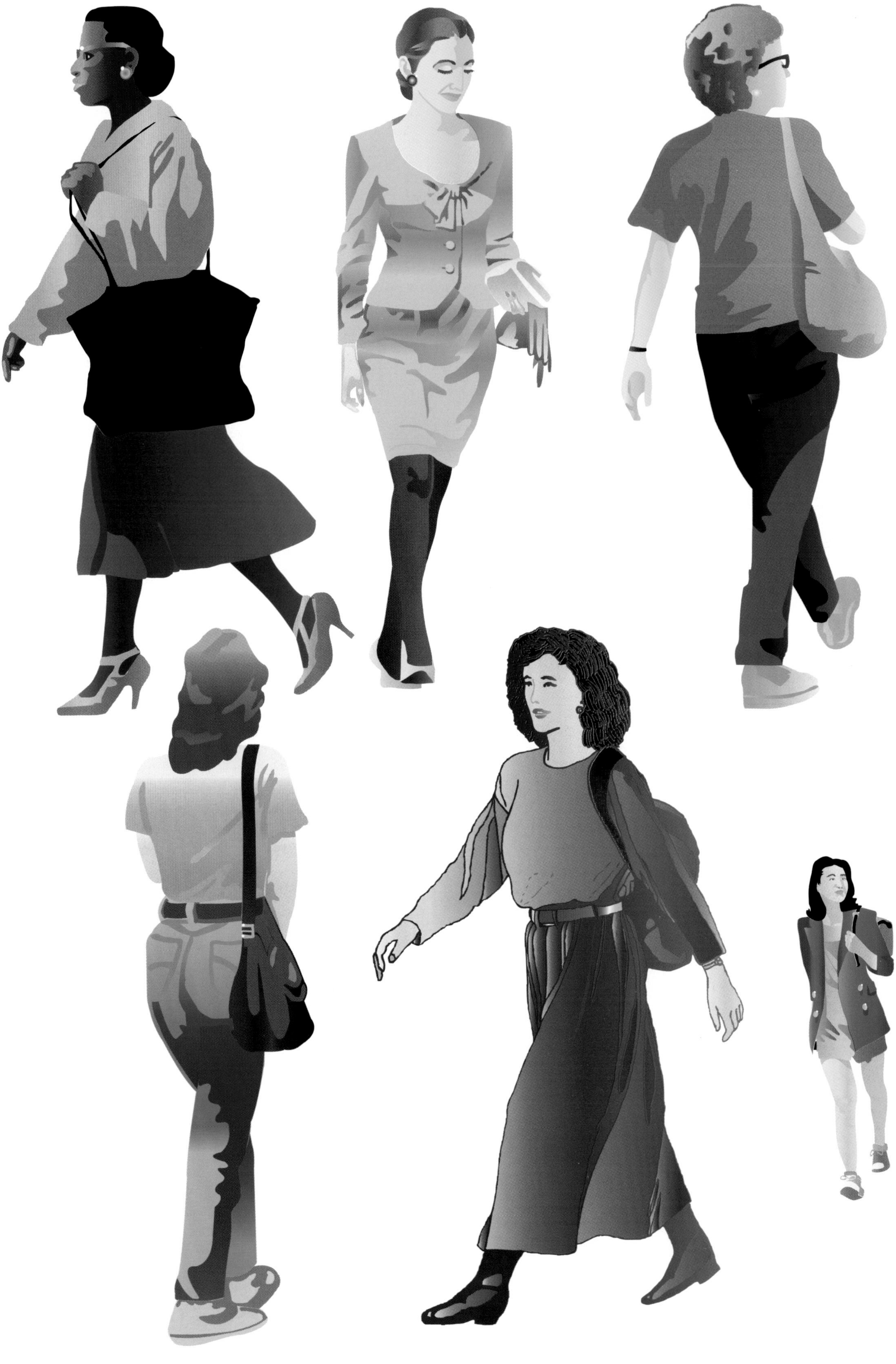

55

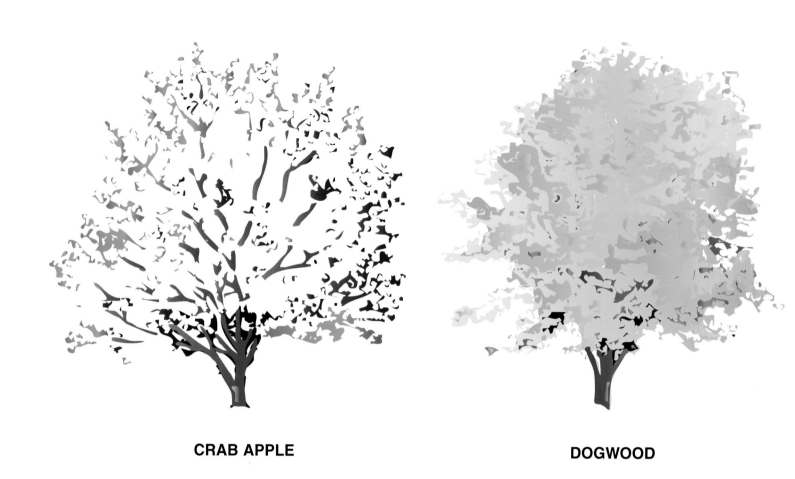

CRAB APPLE

DOGWOOD

HEMLOCK

LONDON PLANE

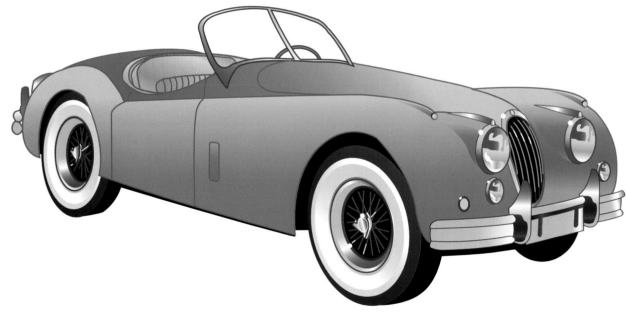

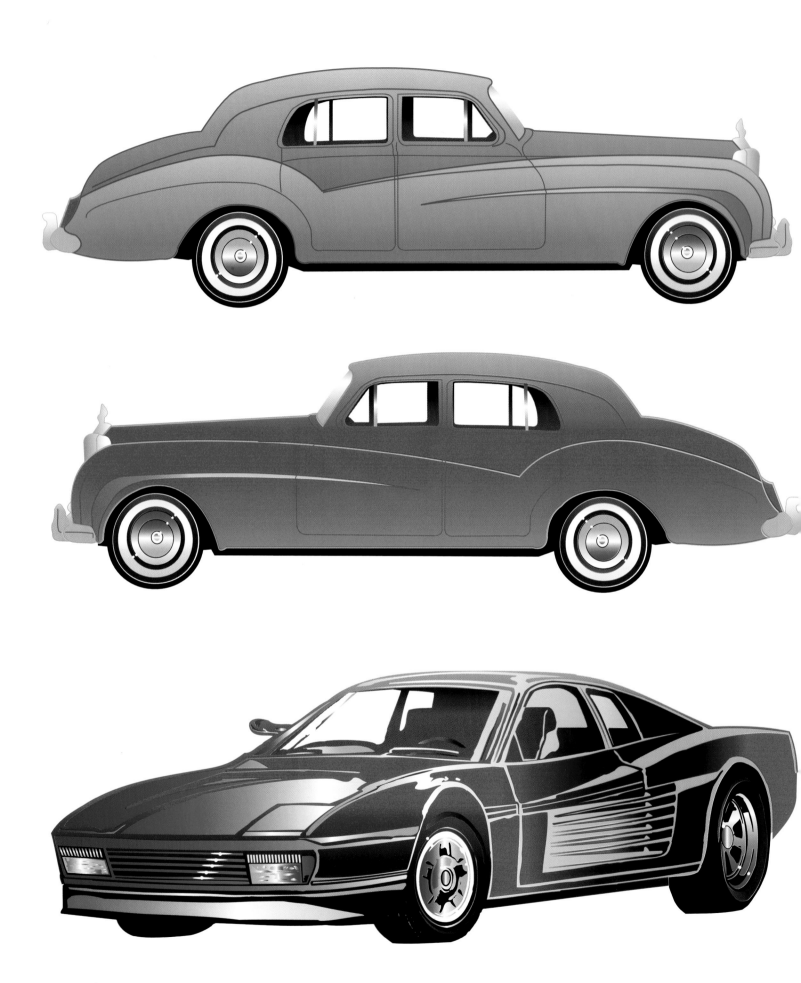

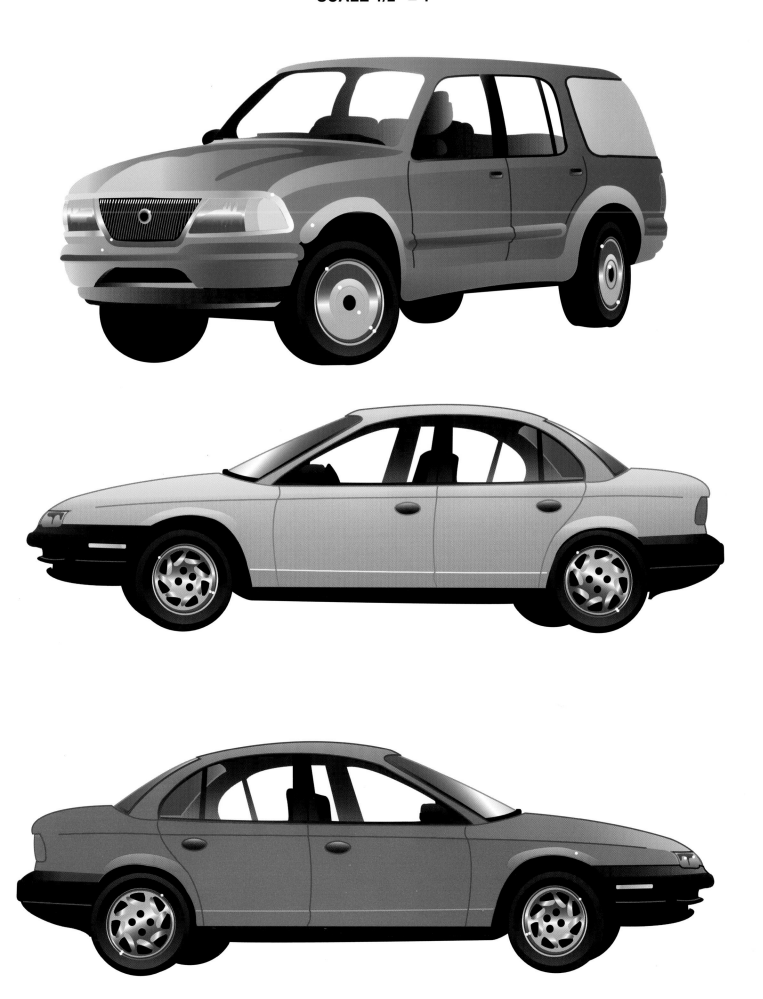

The color section was created in Adobe Illustrator™ 5.5 and 6.0
using an Apple Macintosh Performa 450 with eight megabytes of RAM.

FIGURES

FEMALES

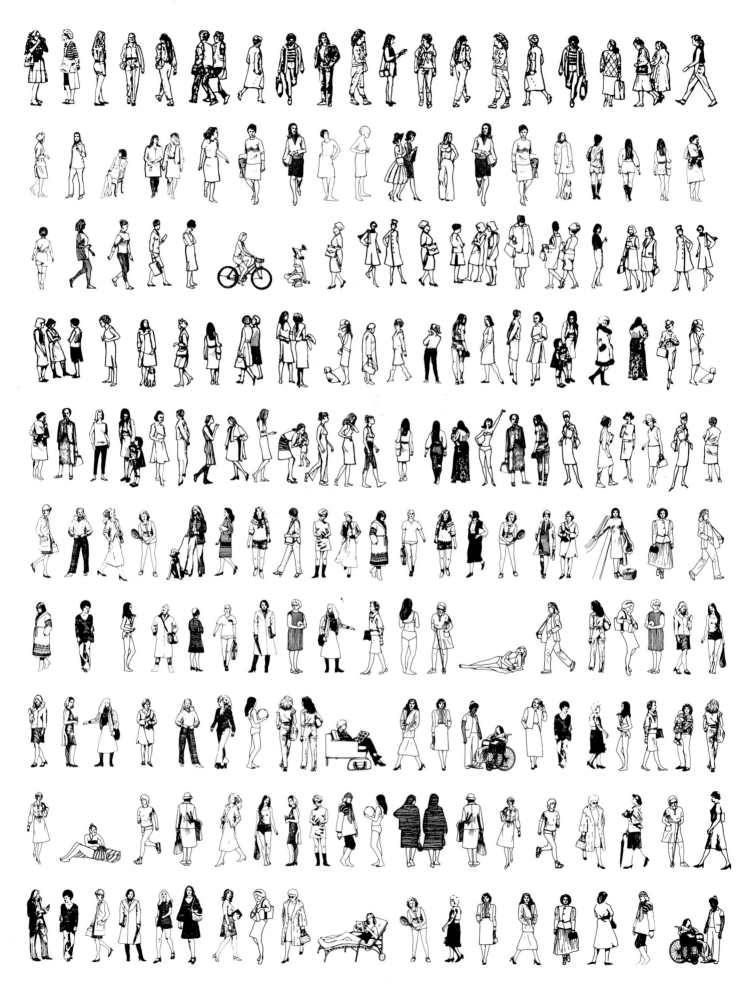

92

FIGURES

MALES

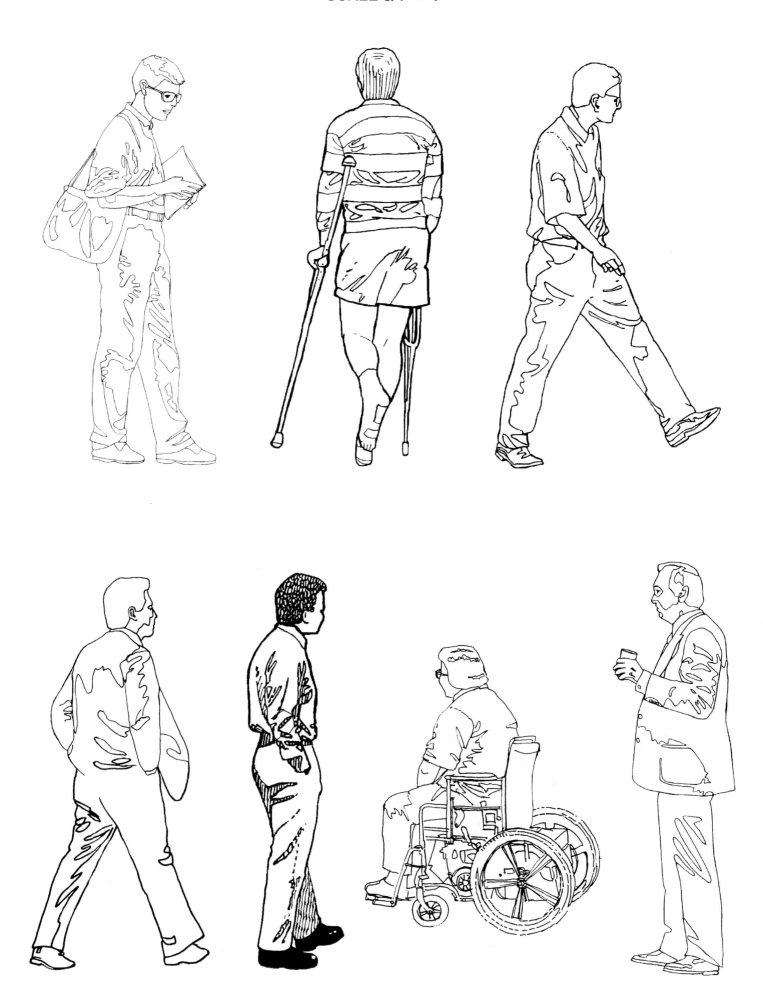

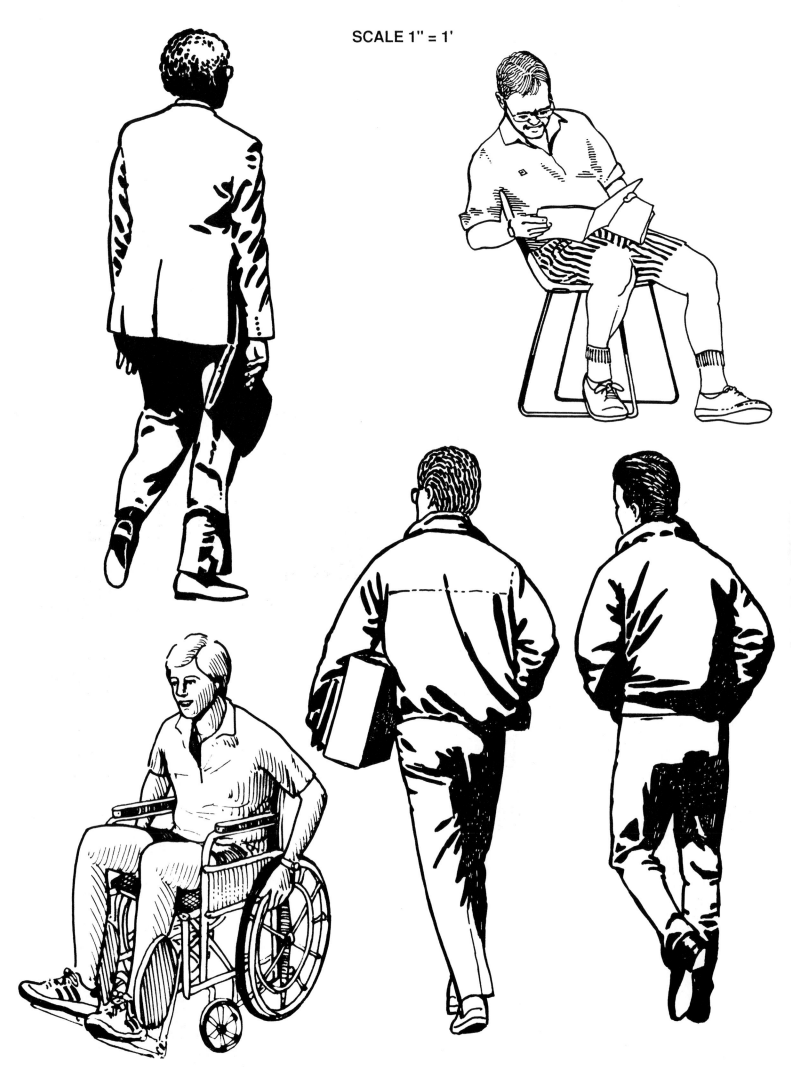

SCALE 1" = 1'

116

FIGURES
GROUPS

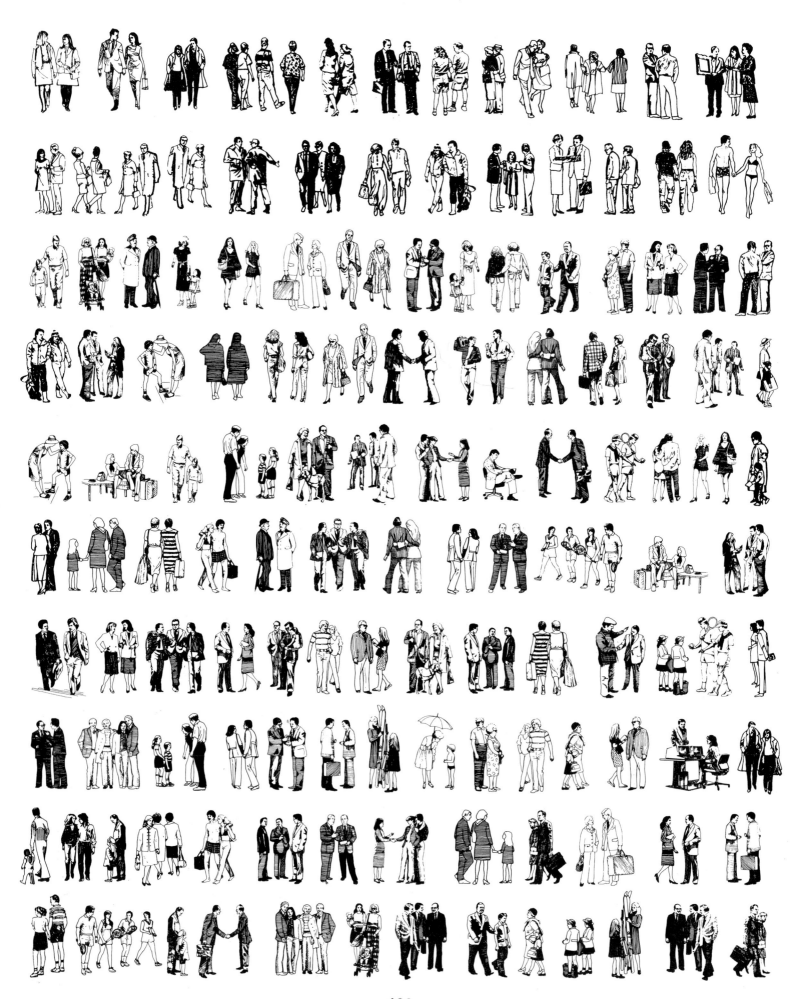

SCALE 1" = 1'

143

SCALE 1" = 1'

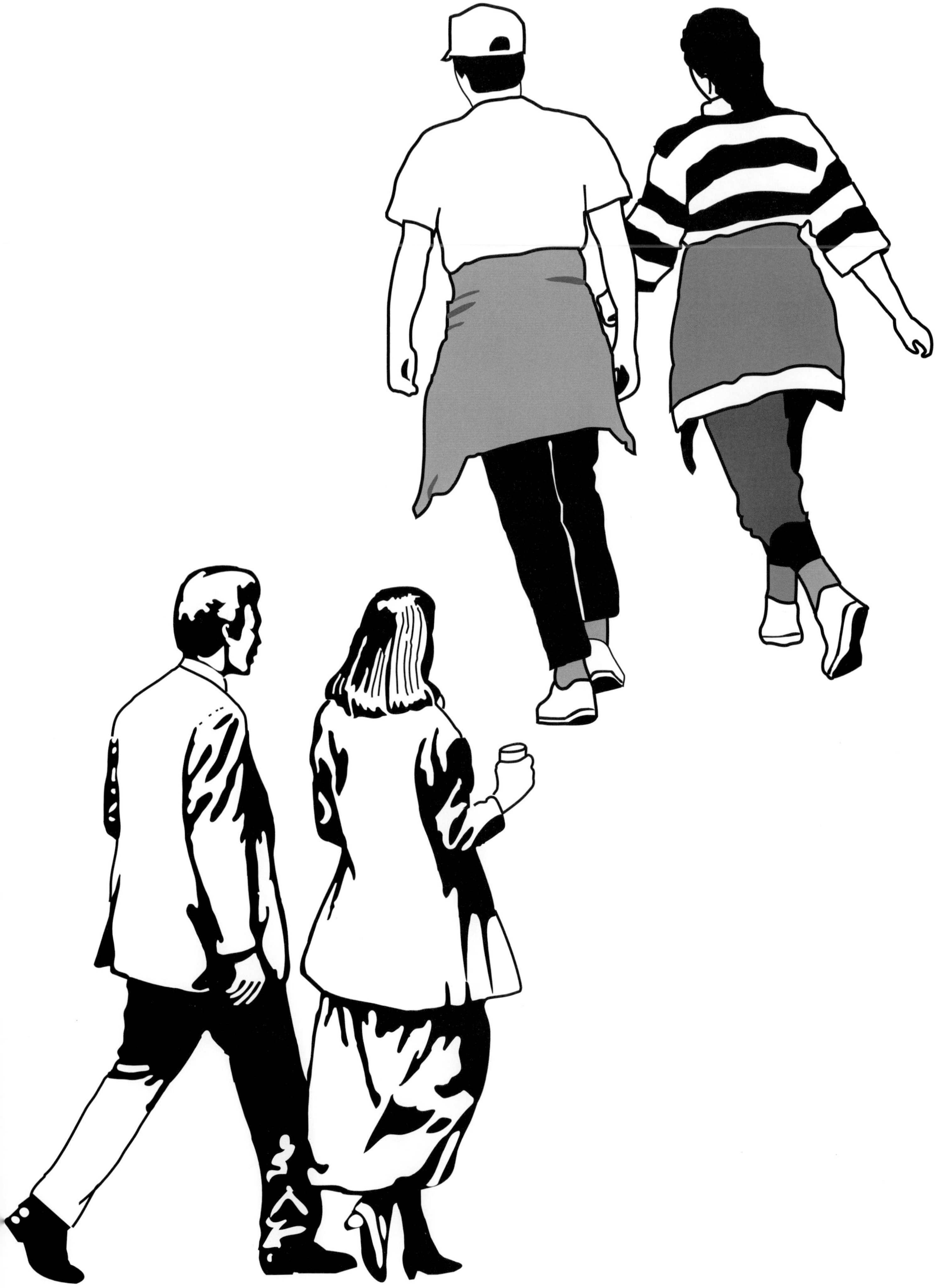

FIGURES
CHILDREN

SCALE 1/8" = 1'

SCALE 1/4" = 1'

148

153

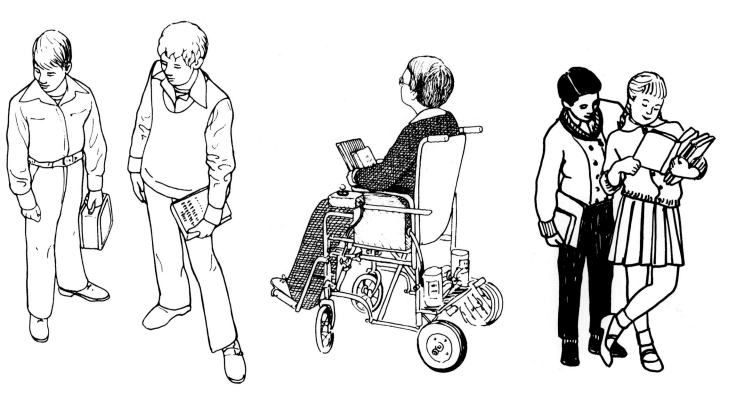

226

JUST
SAY
NO

TREES

GINKO

LINDEN

SWEET GUM

PIN OAK

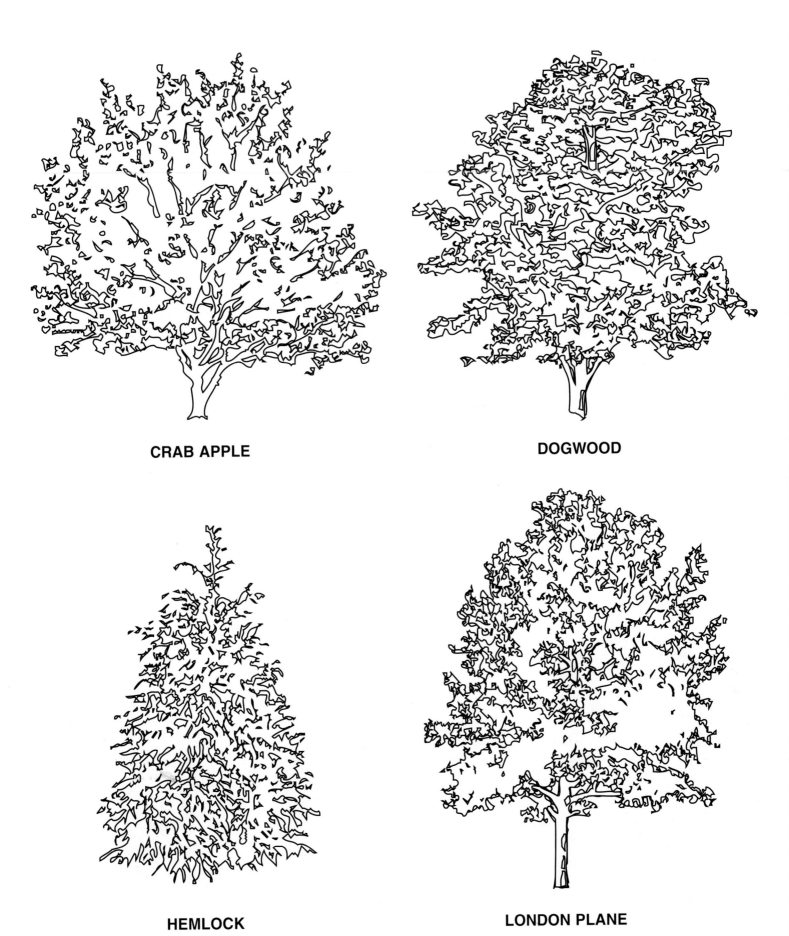

CRAB APPLE

DOGWOOD

HEMLOCK

LONDON PLANE

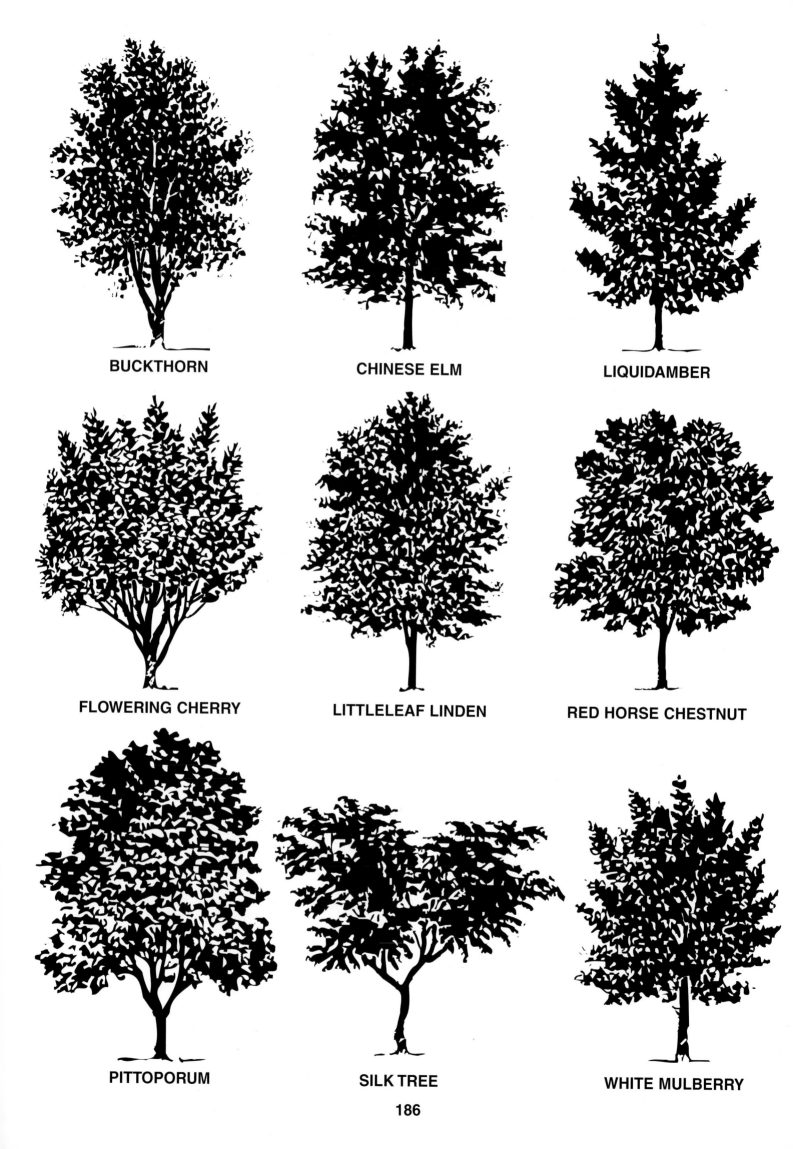

BUCKTHORN

CHINESE ELM

LIQUIDAMBER

FLOWERING CHERRY

LITTLELEAF LINDEN

RED HORSE CHESTNUT

PITTOPORUM

SILK TREE

WHITE MULBERRY

186

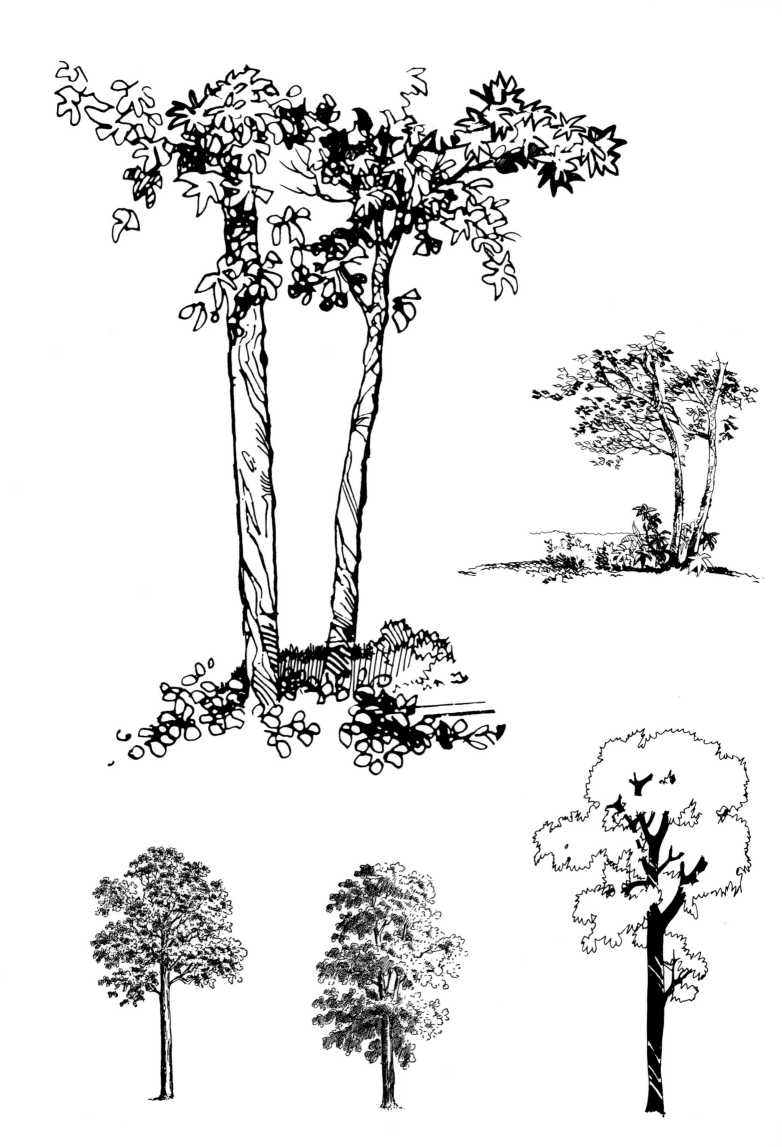

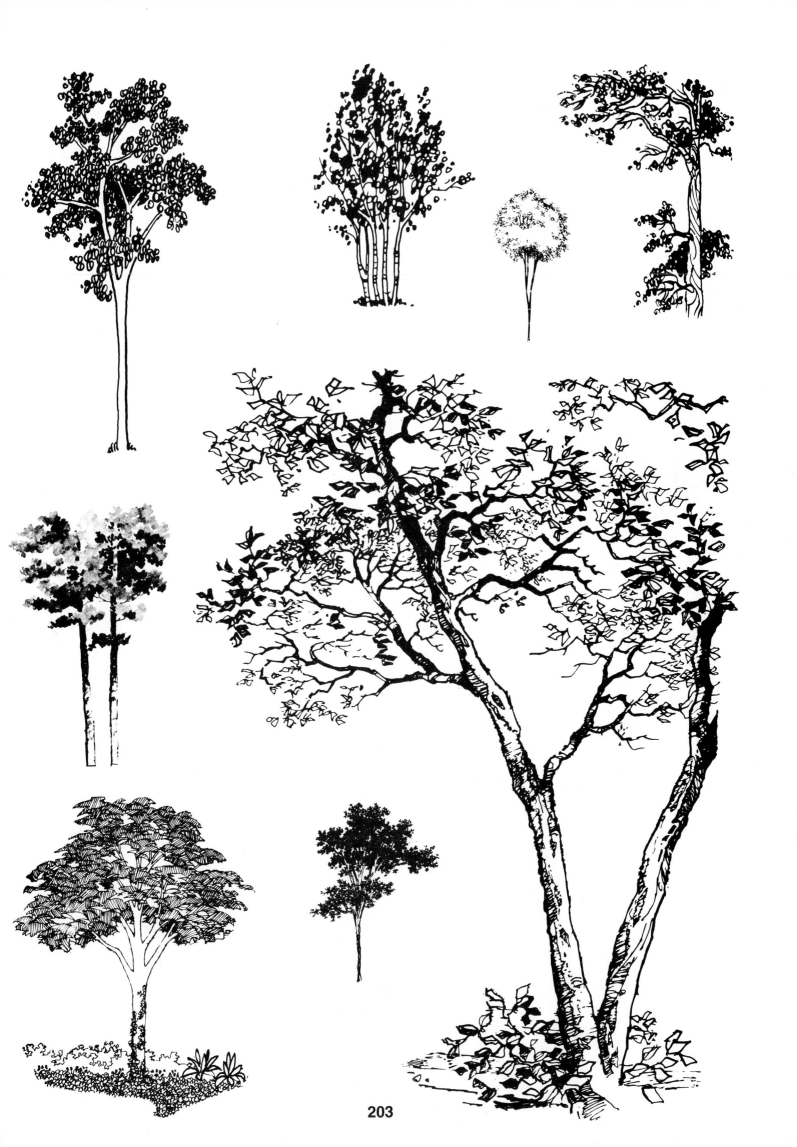

206

209

214

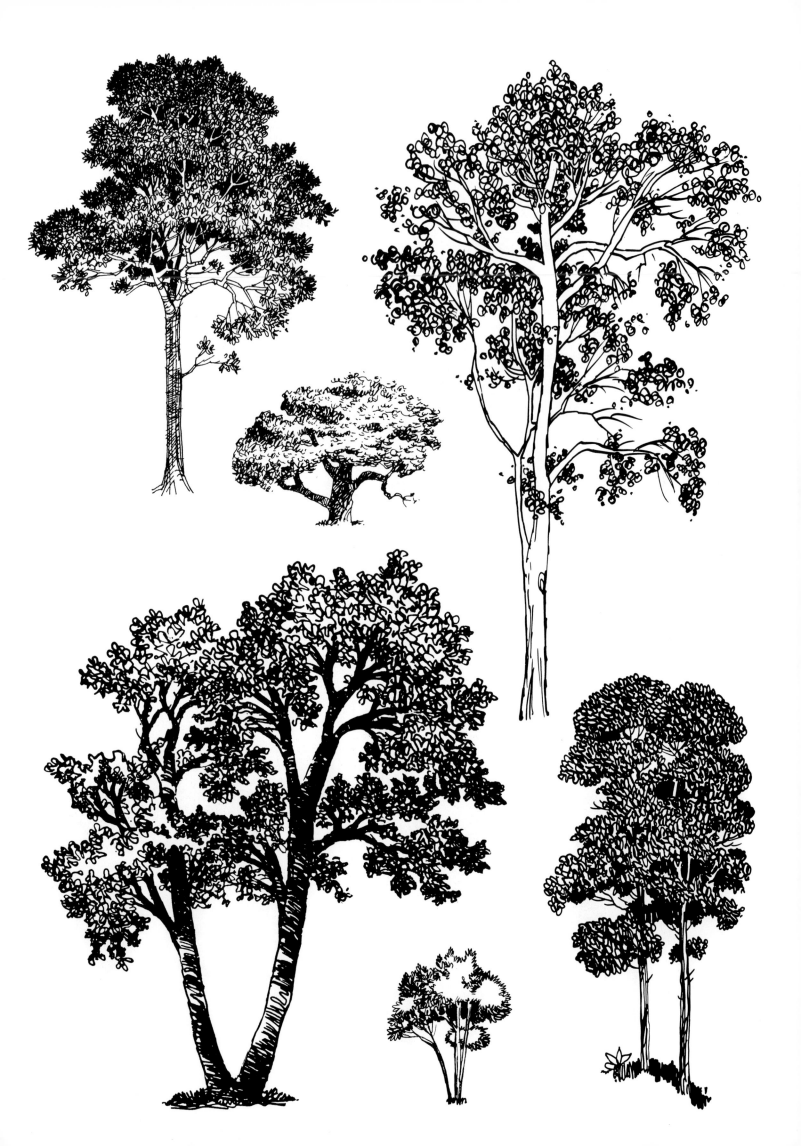

222

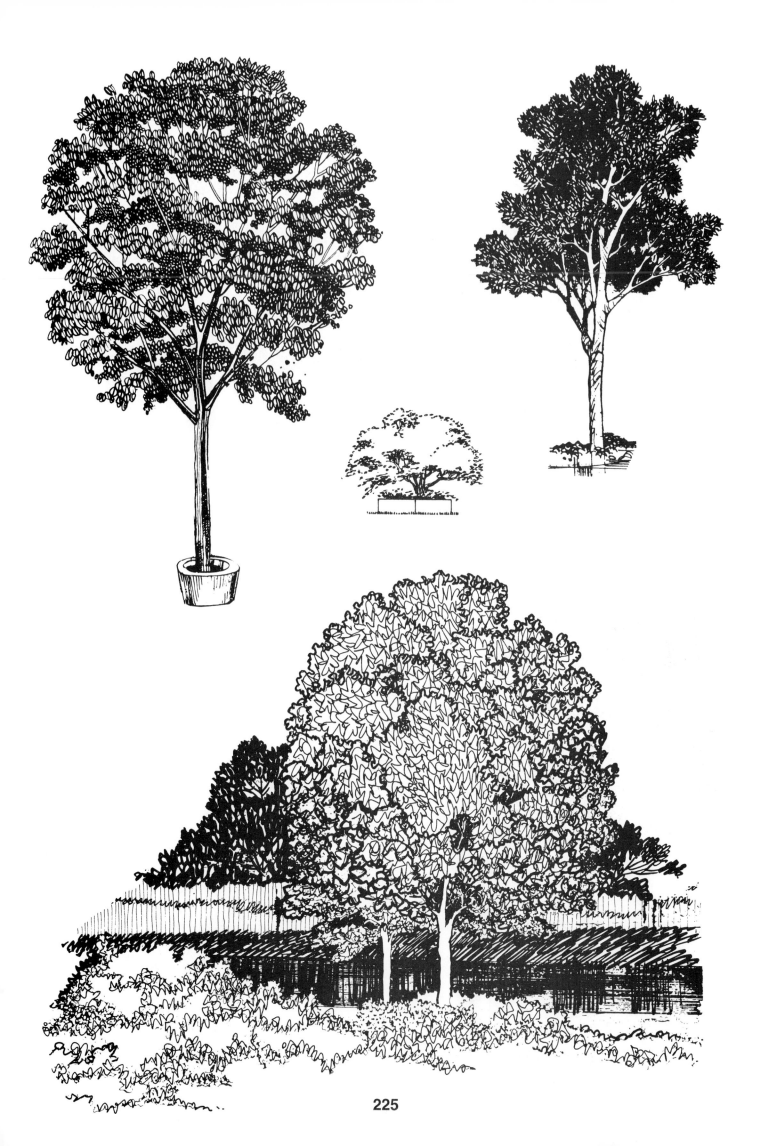

228

233

239

242

244

248

251

252

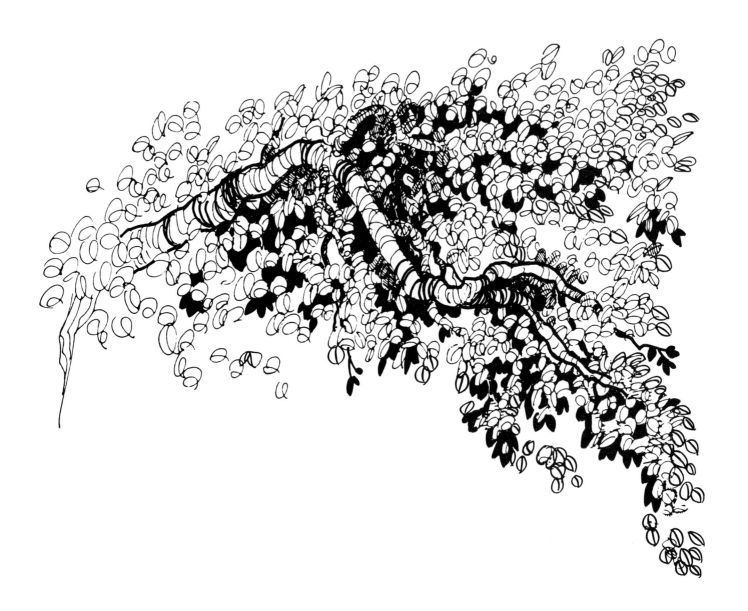

256

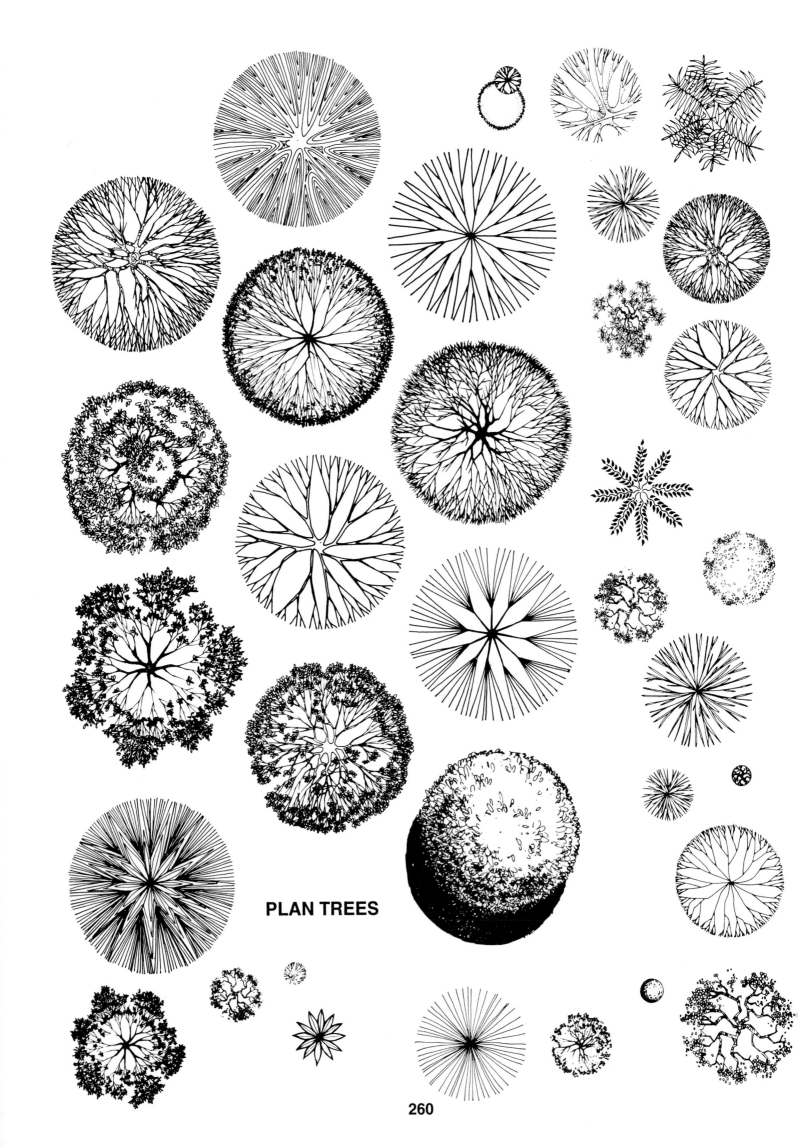

PLAN TREES

260

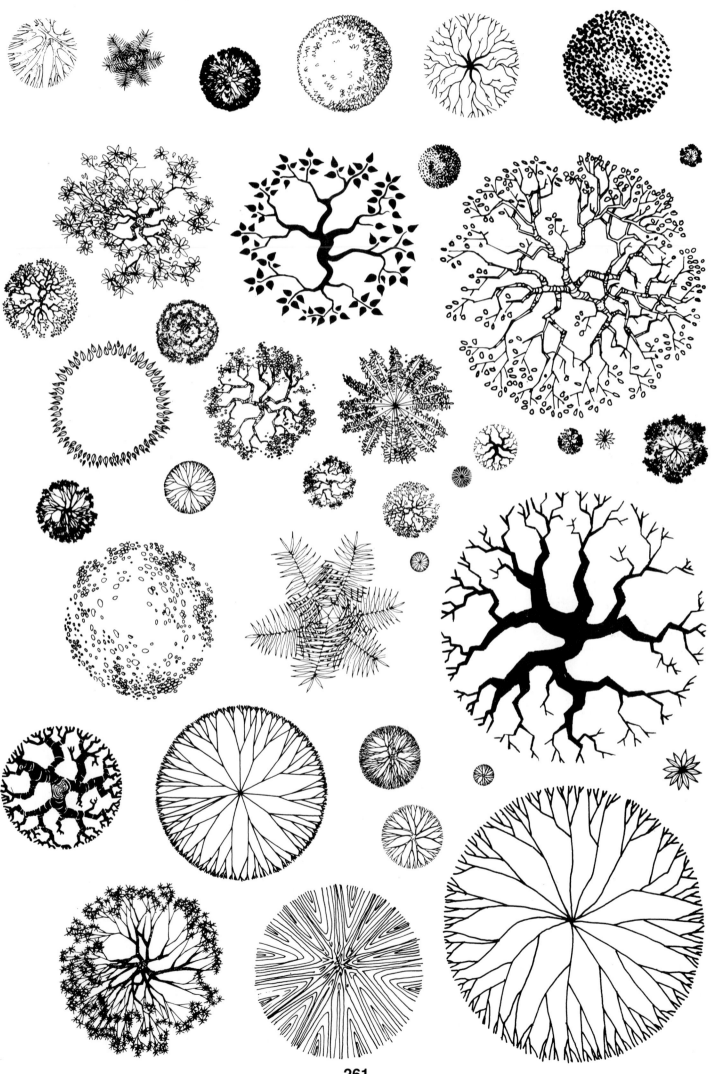

PLANTS

266

272

276

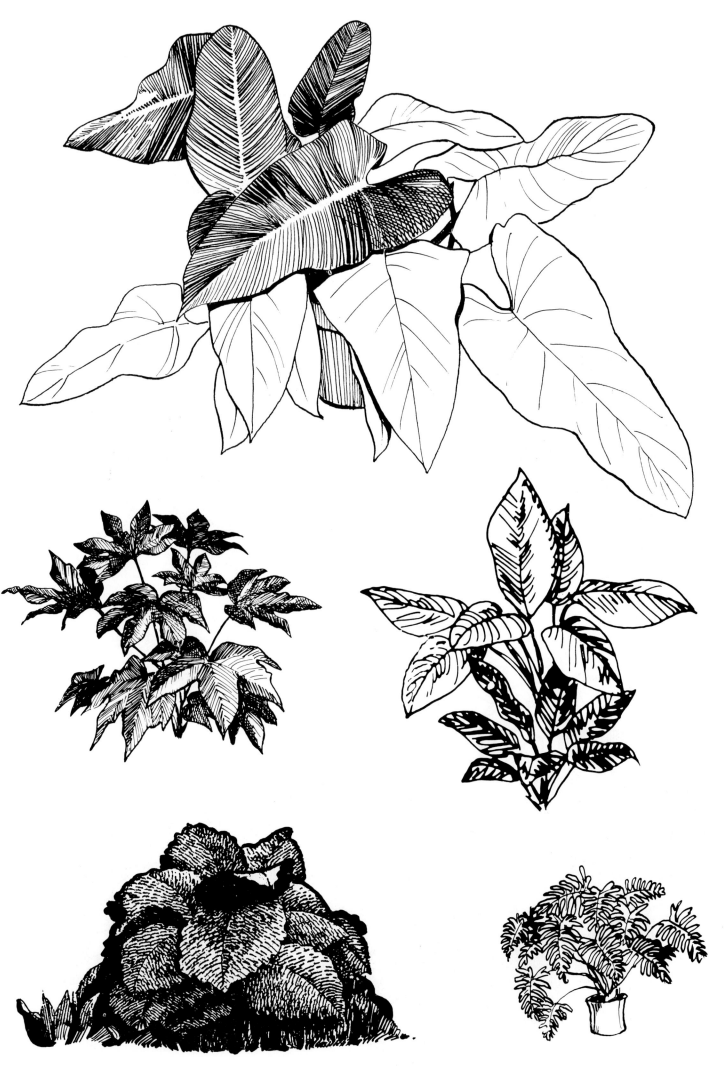

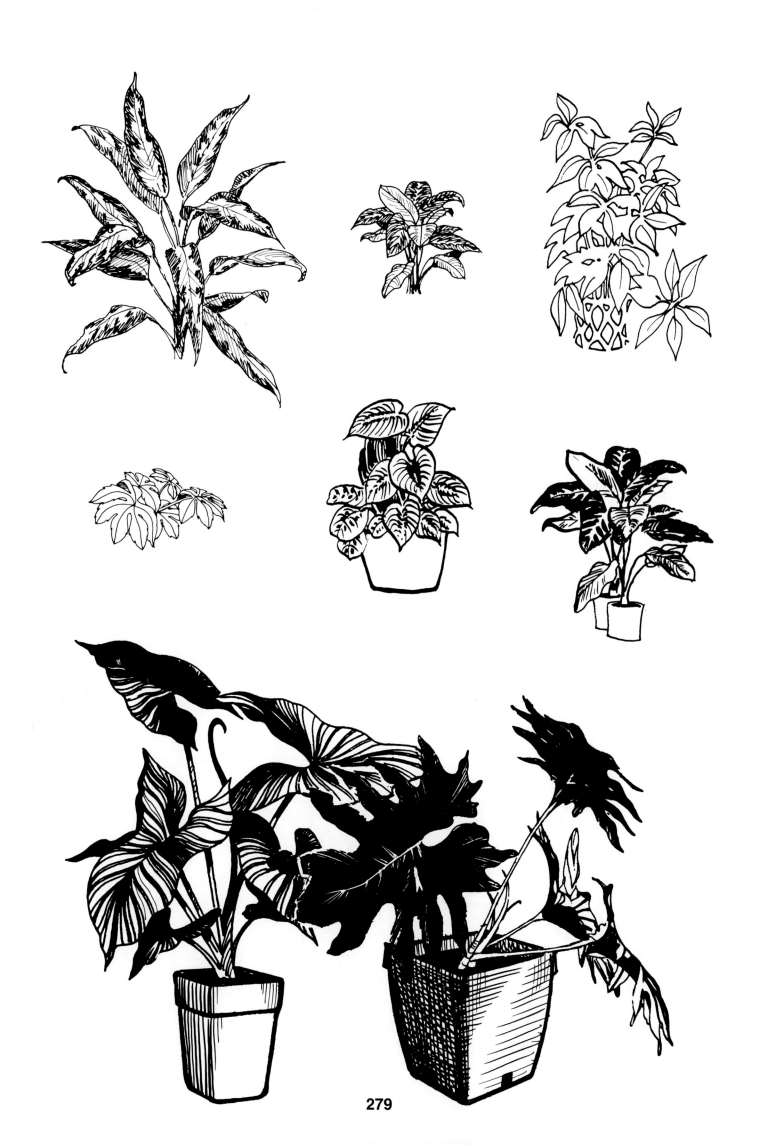

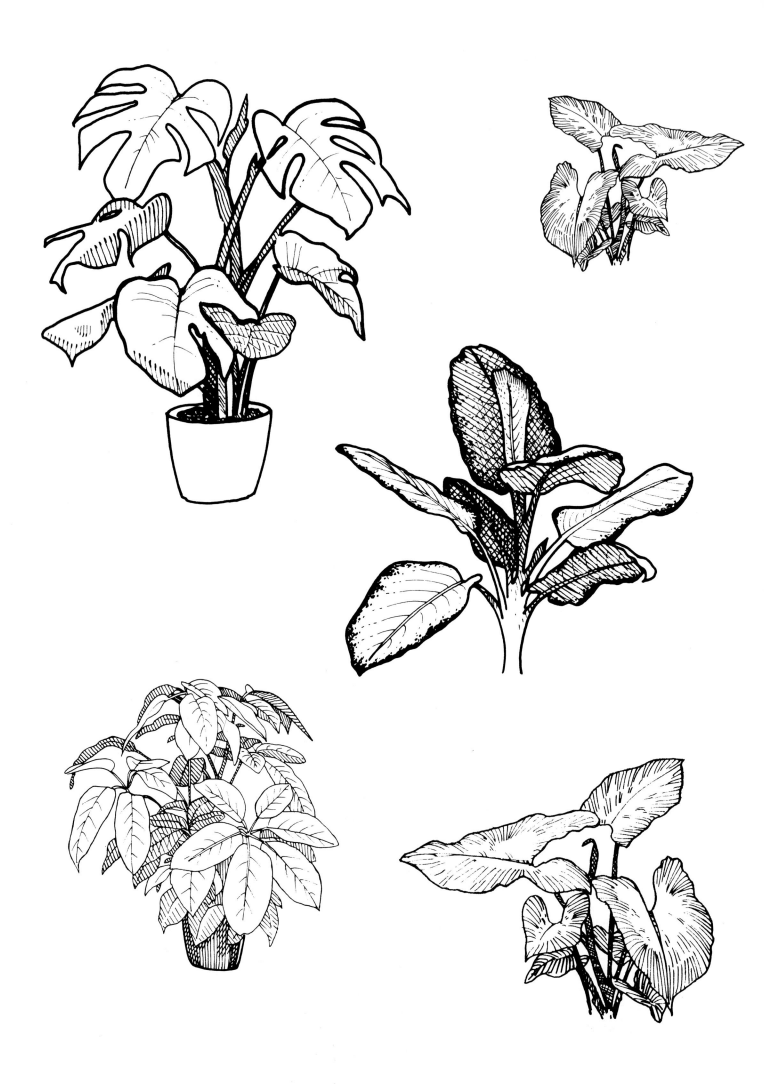

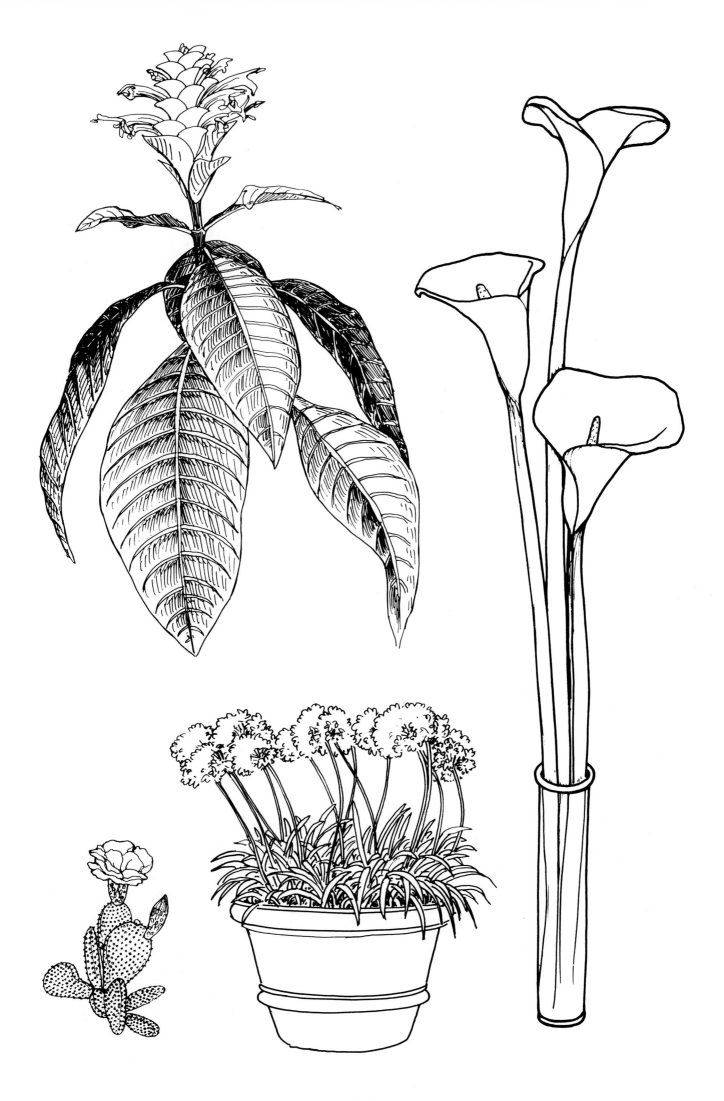

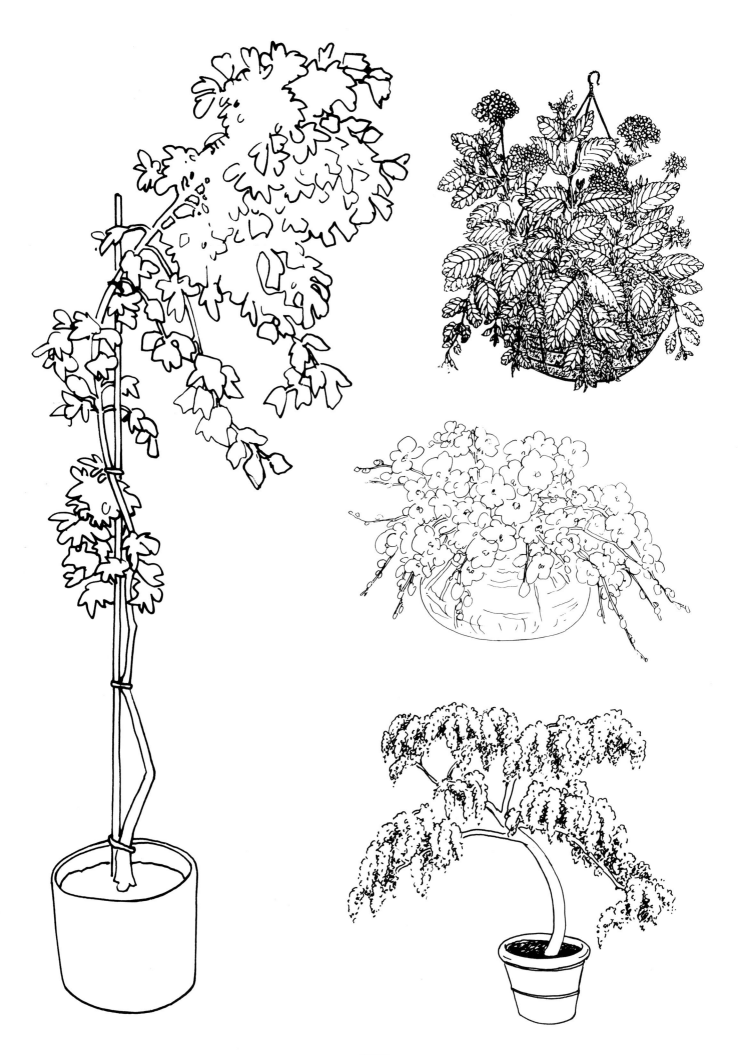

287

288

293

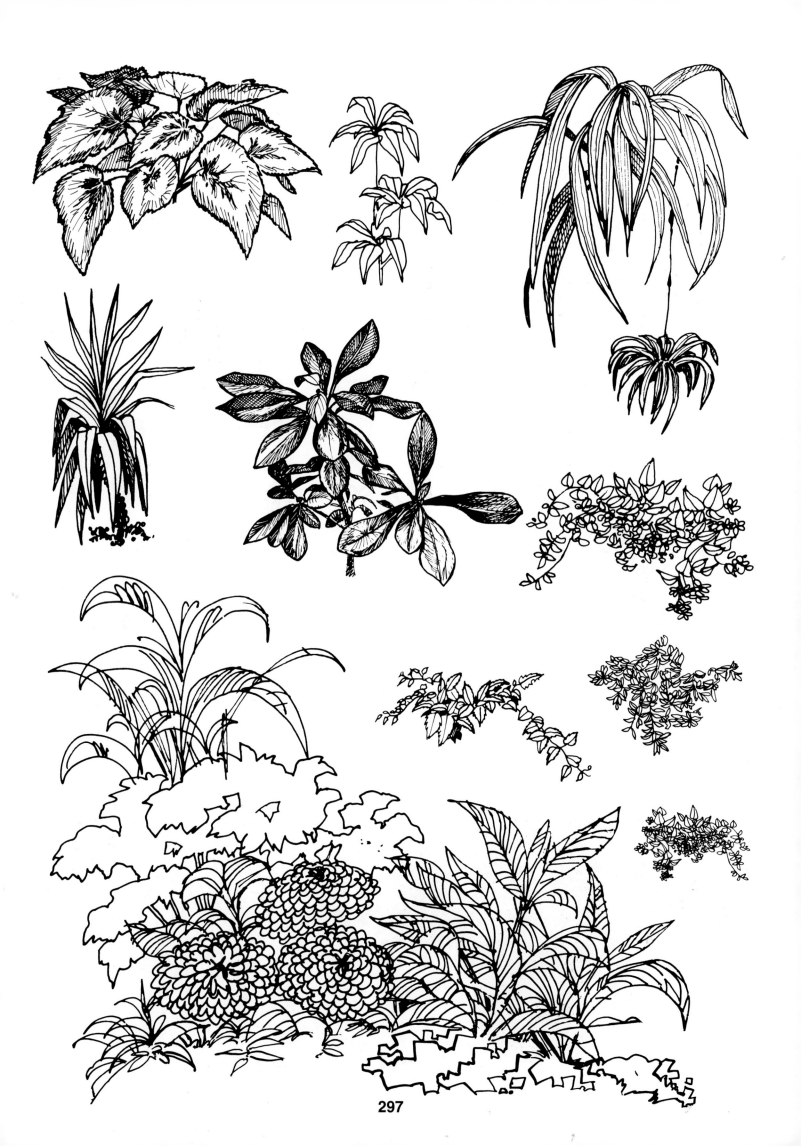

297

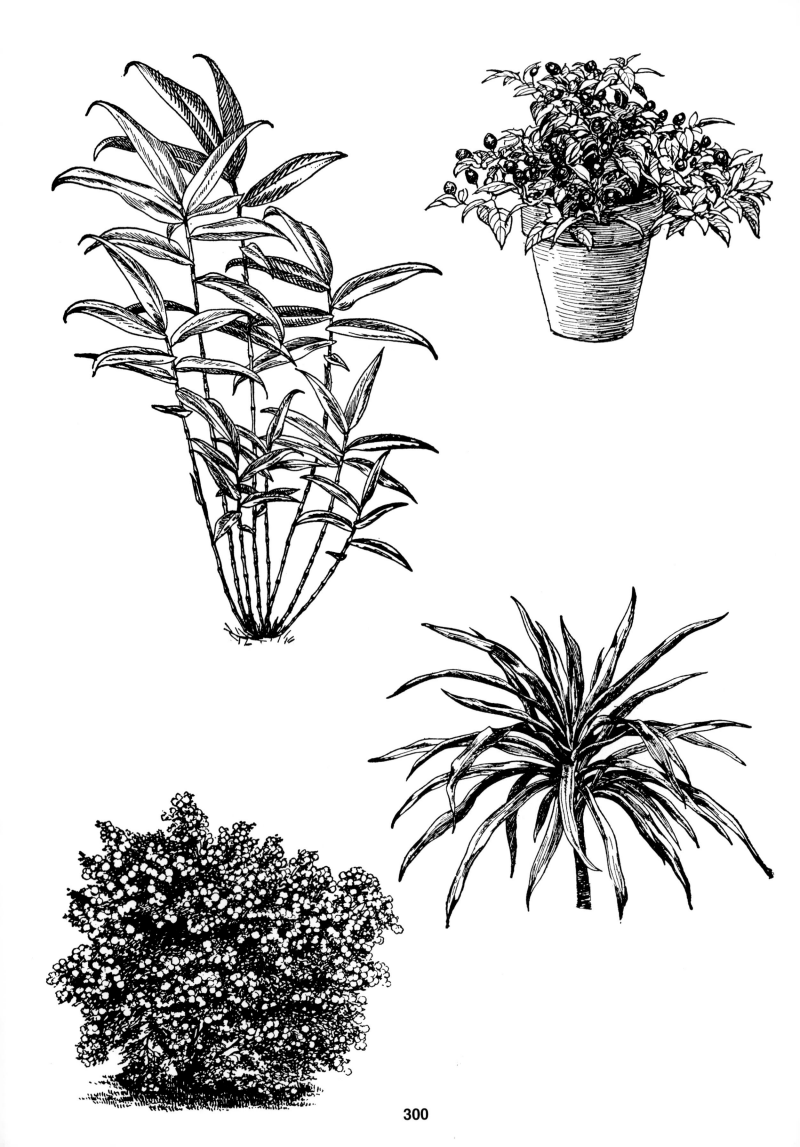

307

VEHICLES

SCALE 1/16" = 1'

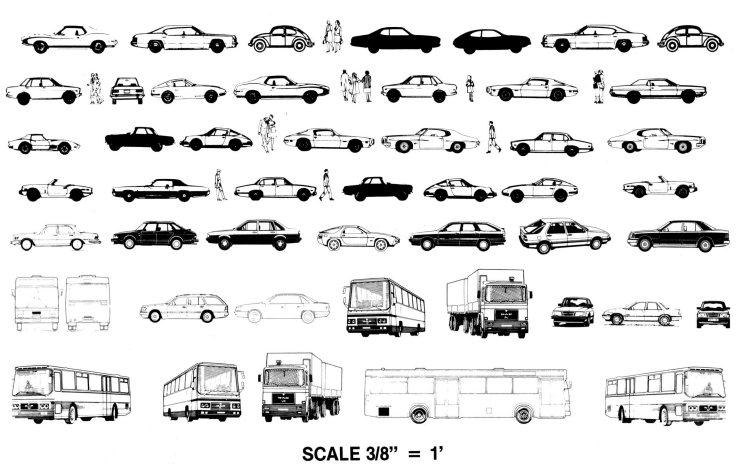

SCALE 3/8" = 1'

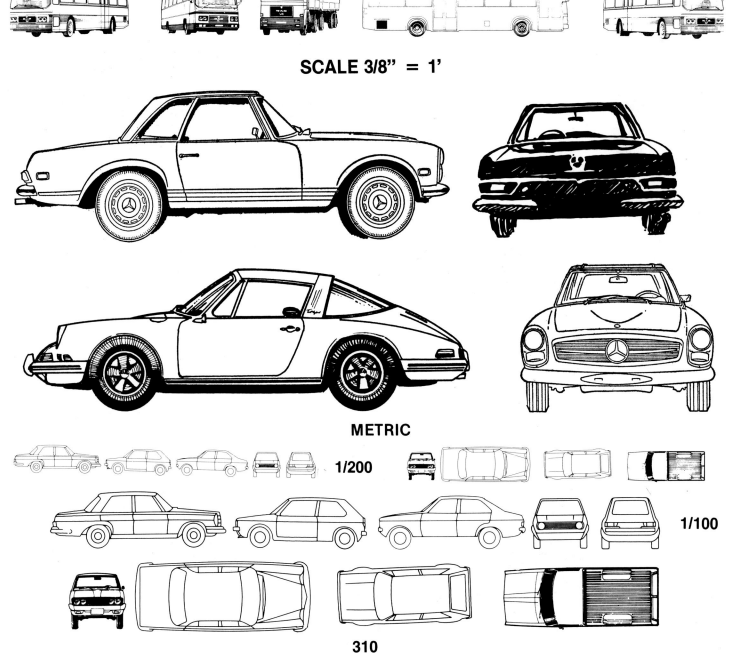

METRIC

1/200

1/100

310

METRIC 1/50

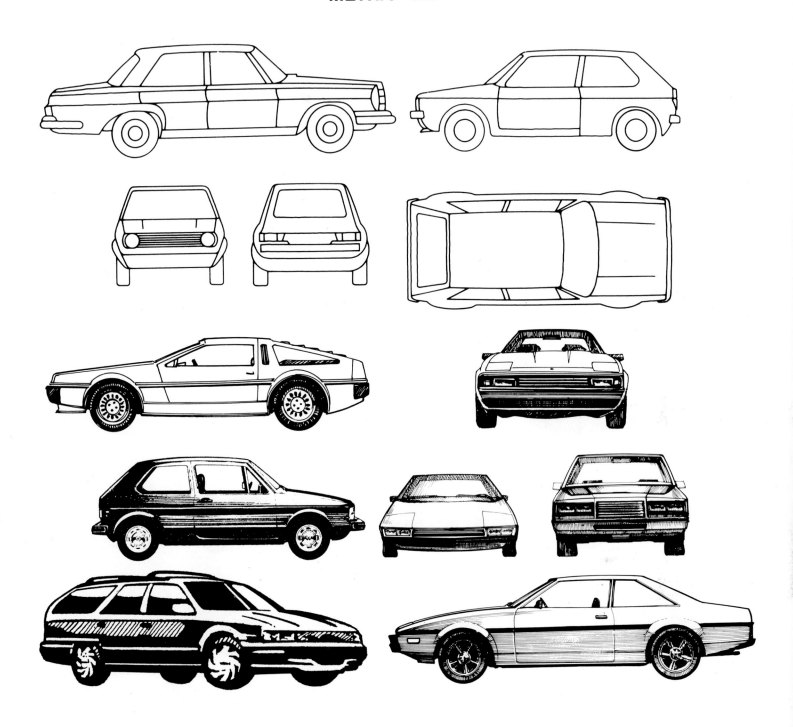

METRIC 1/25

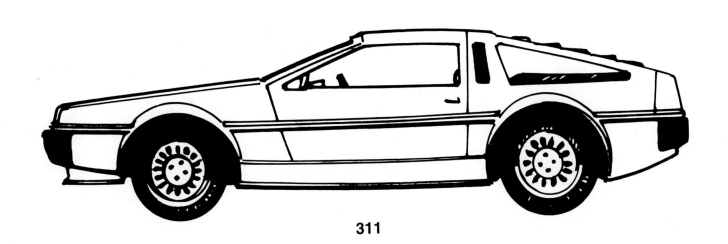

SCALE 3/16"=1'

316

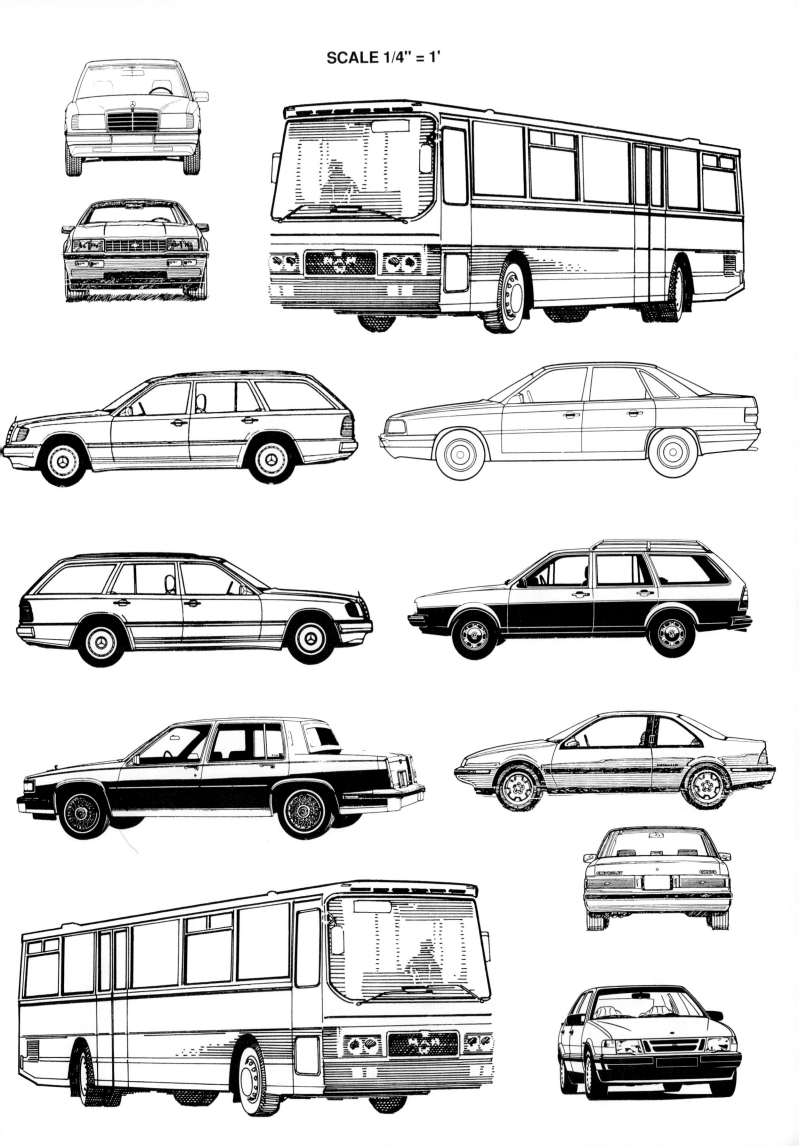

SCALE 1/4" = 1'

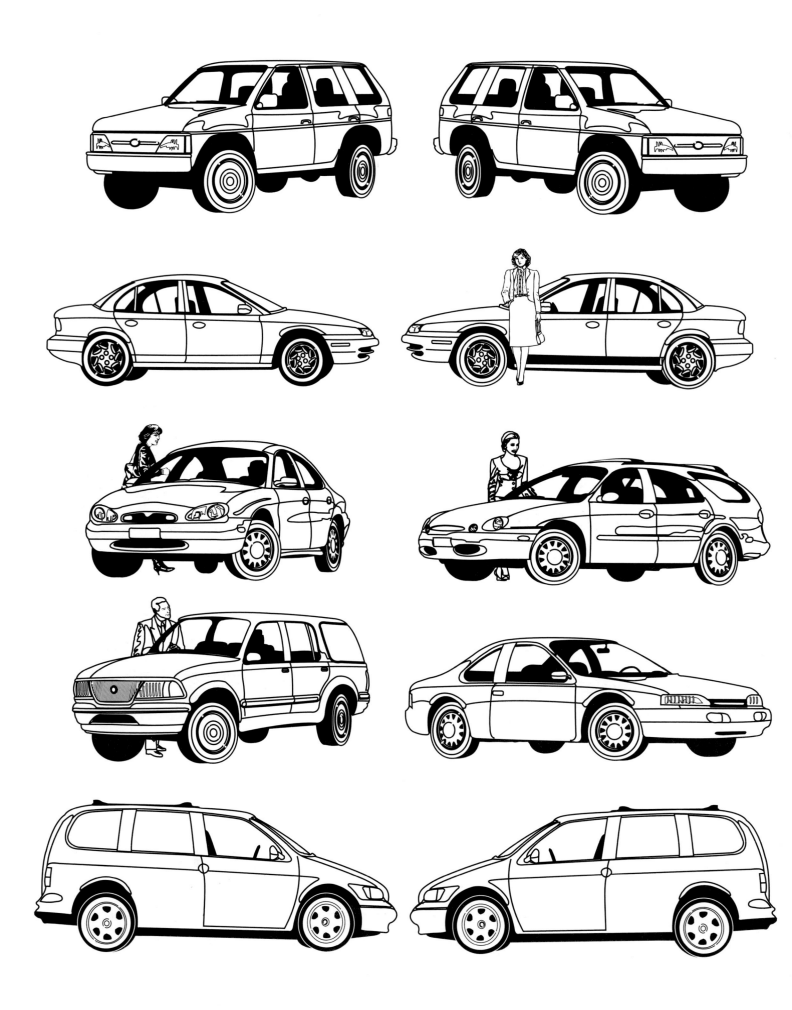

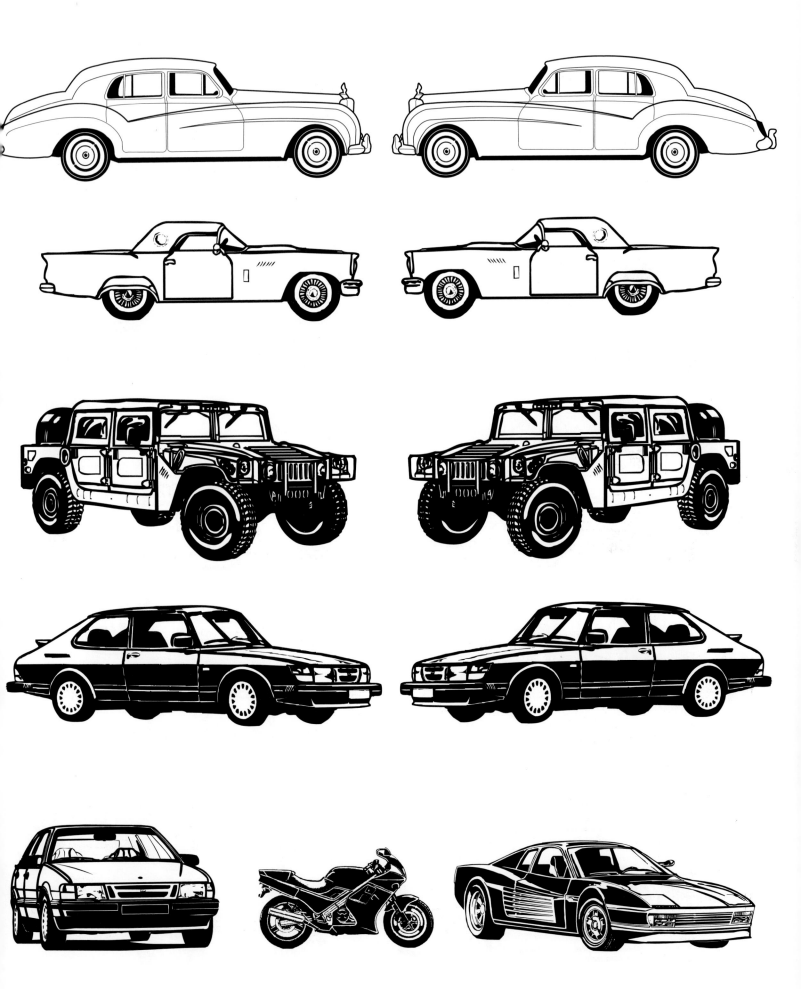

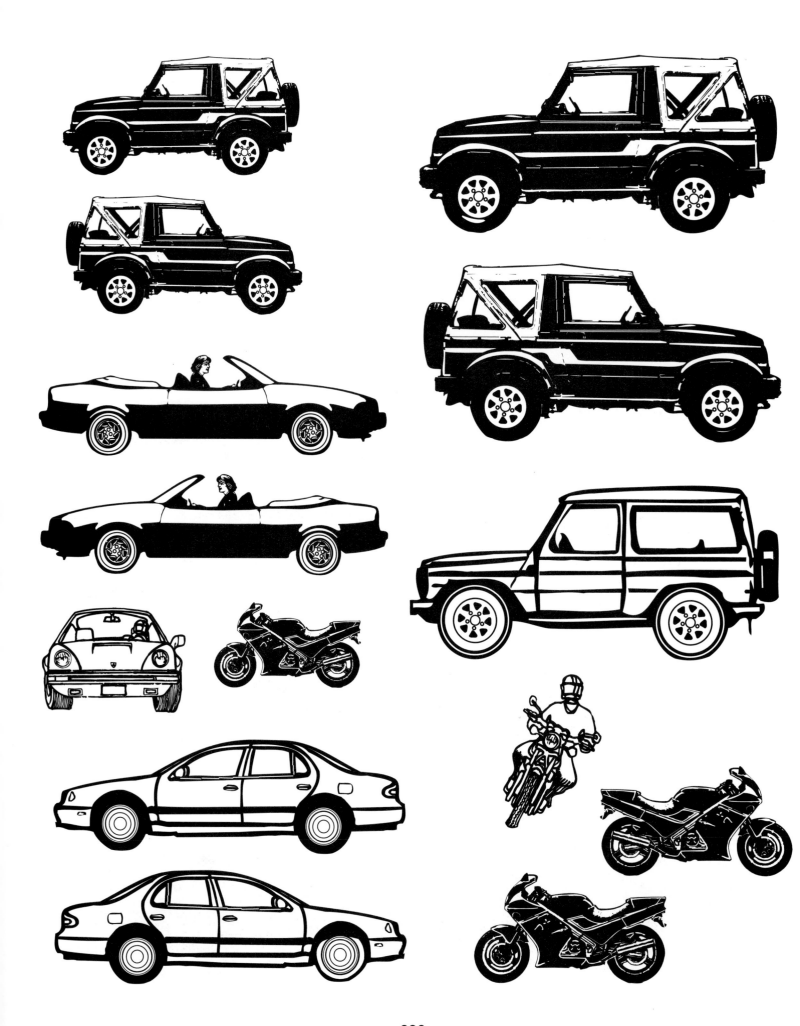

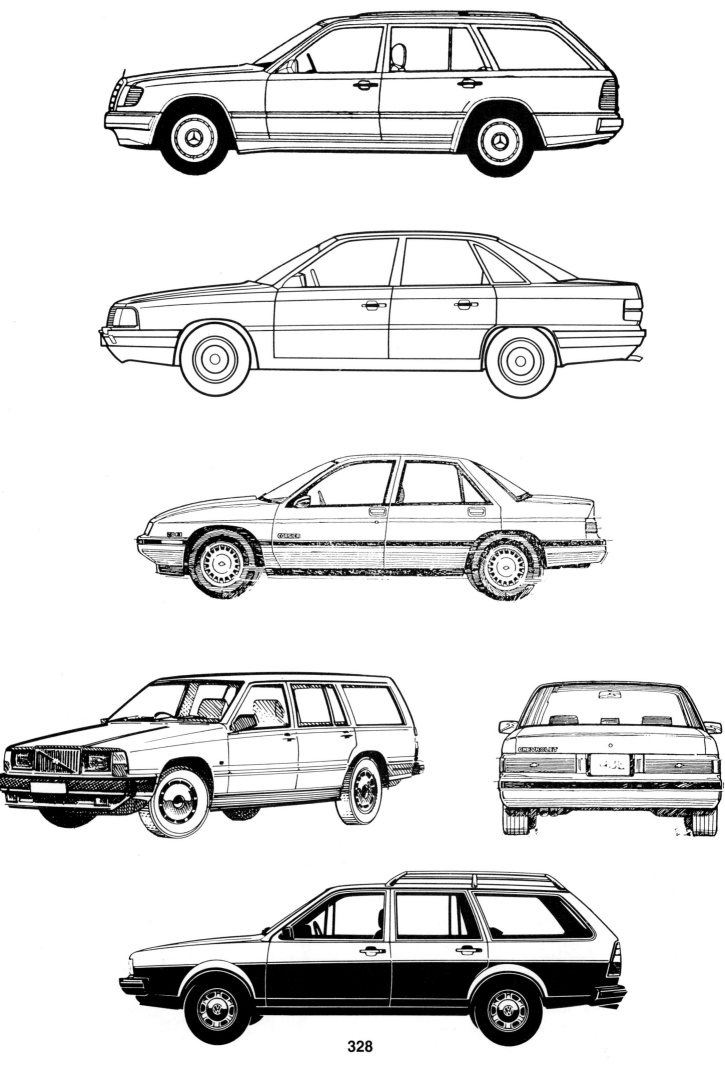

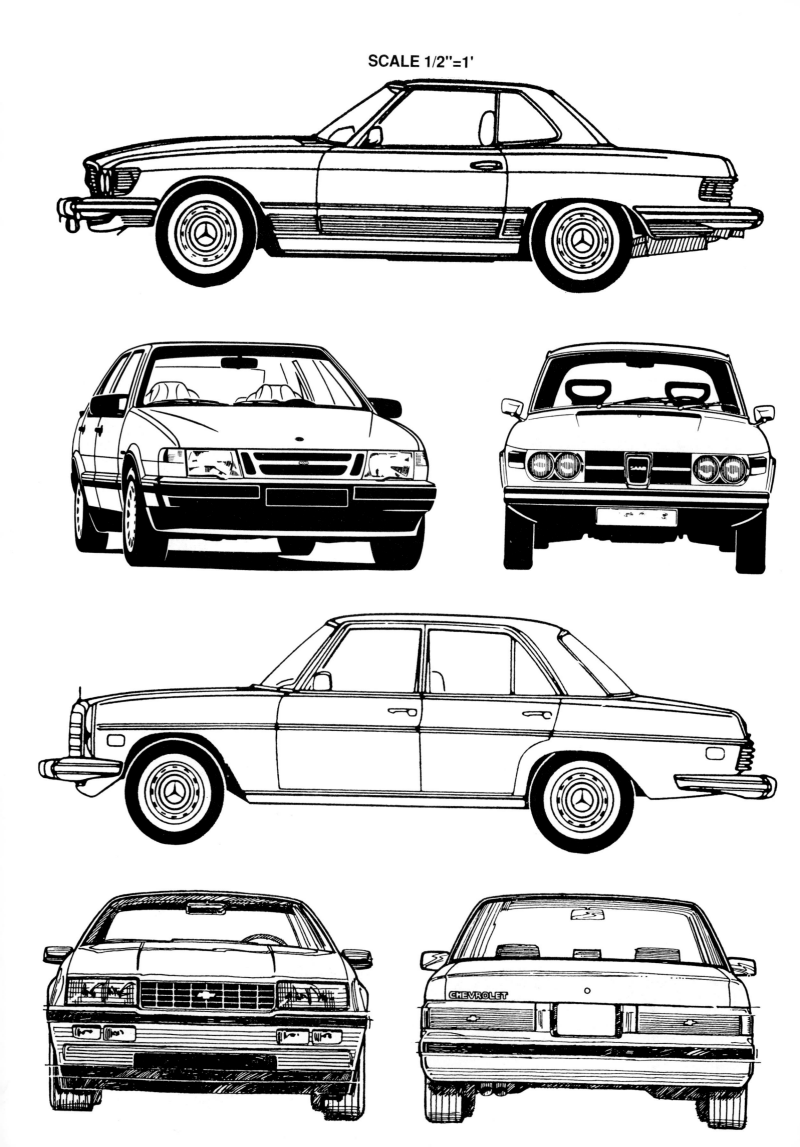

SCALE 1/2"=1'

SCALE 1/2"=1'

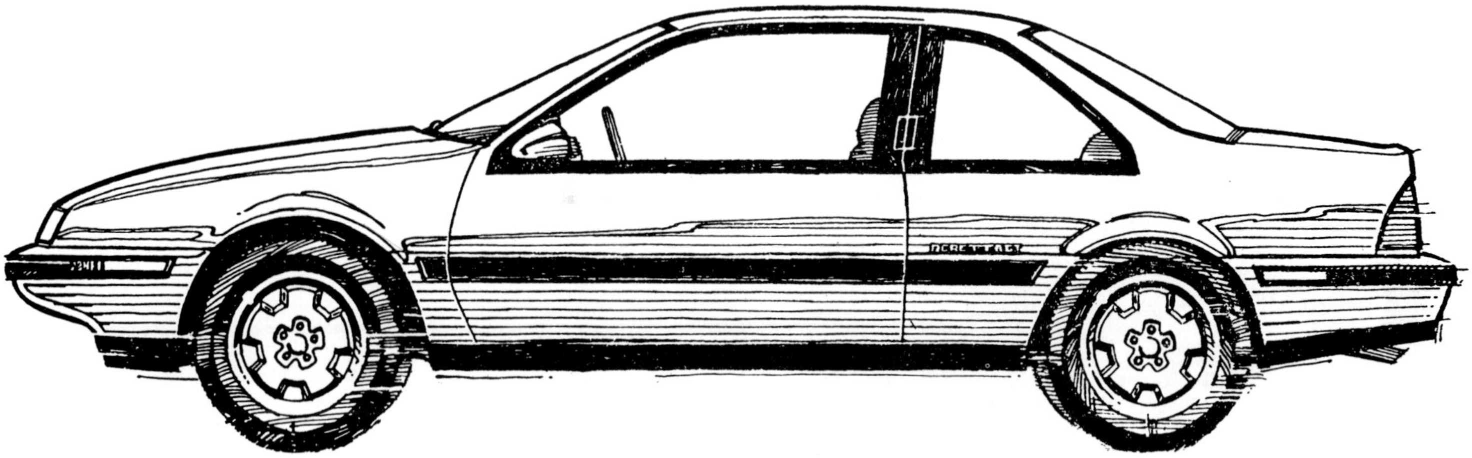

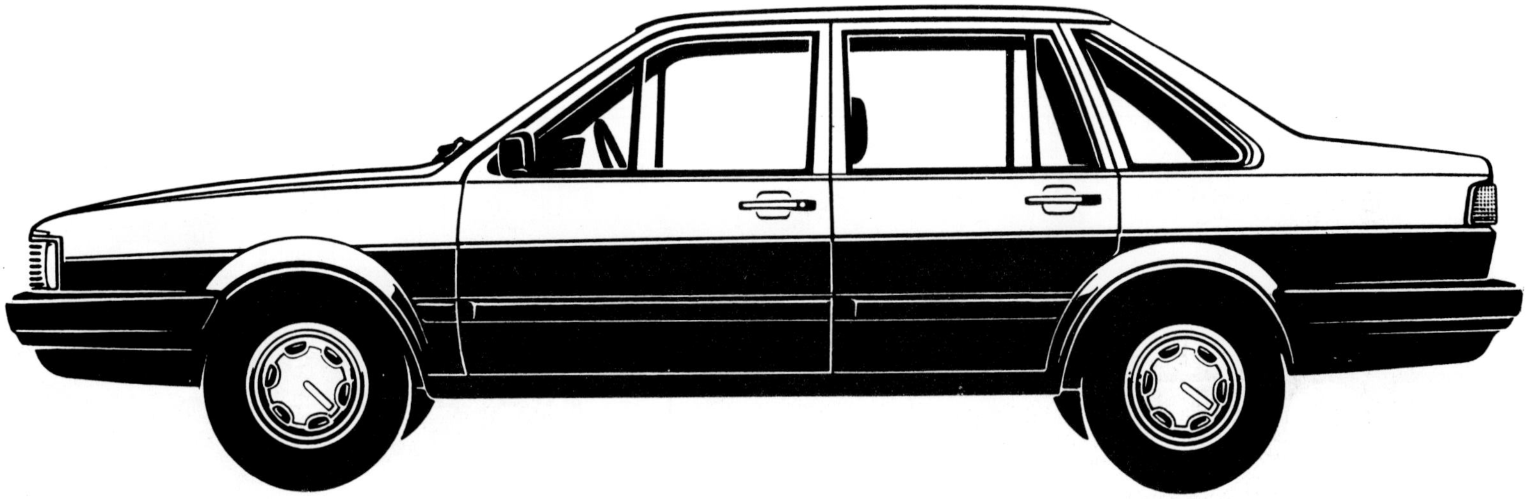

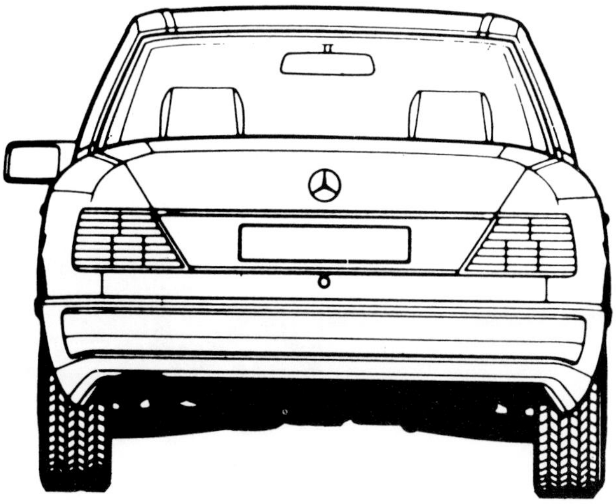

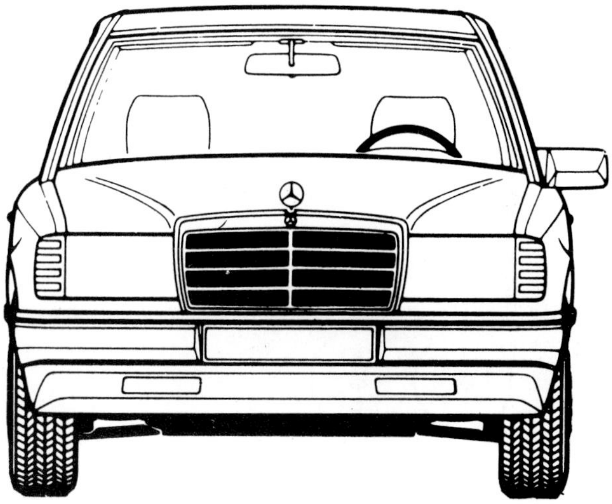

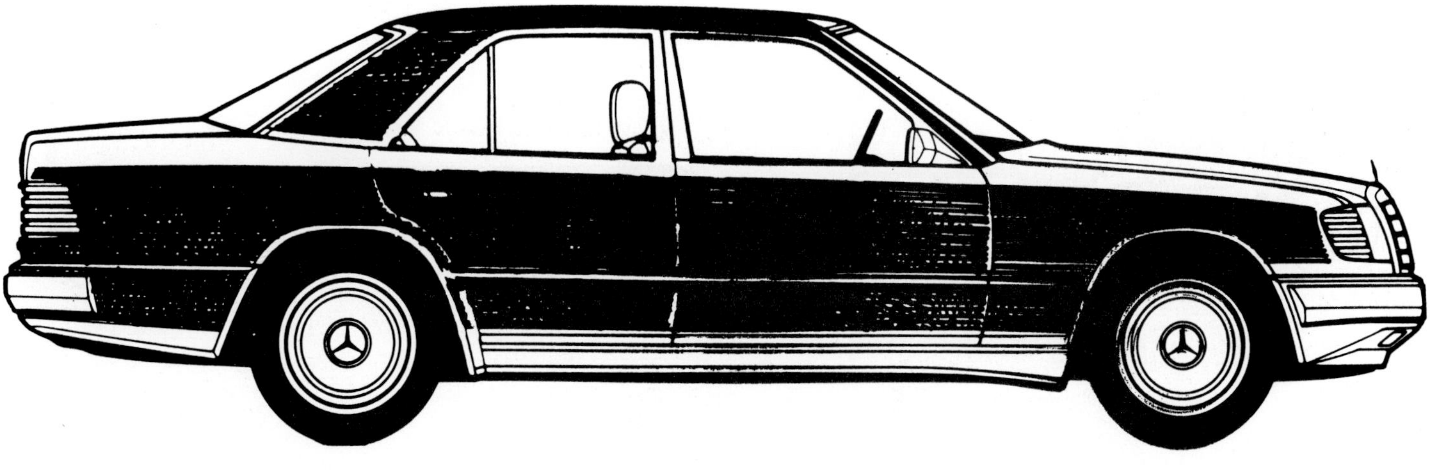

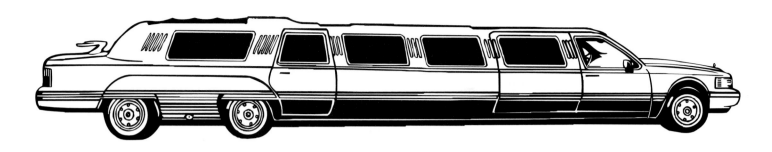

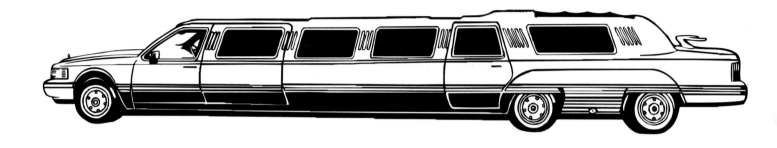

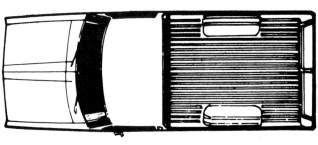

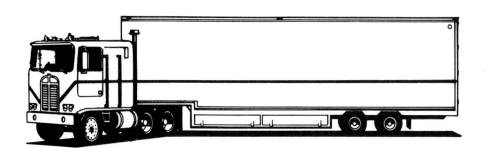

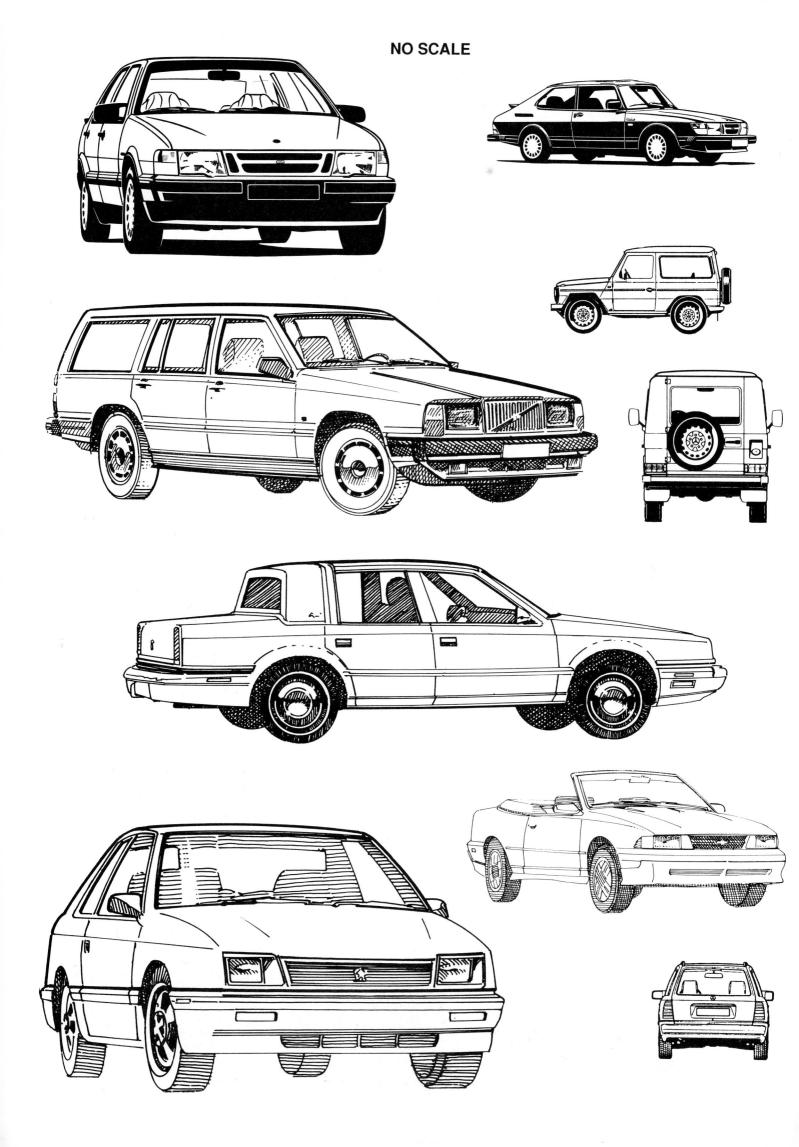

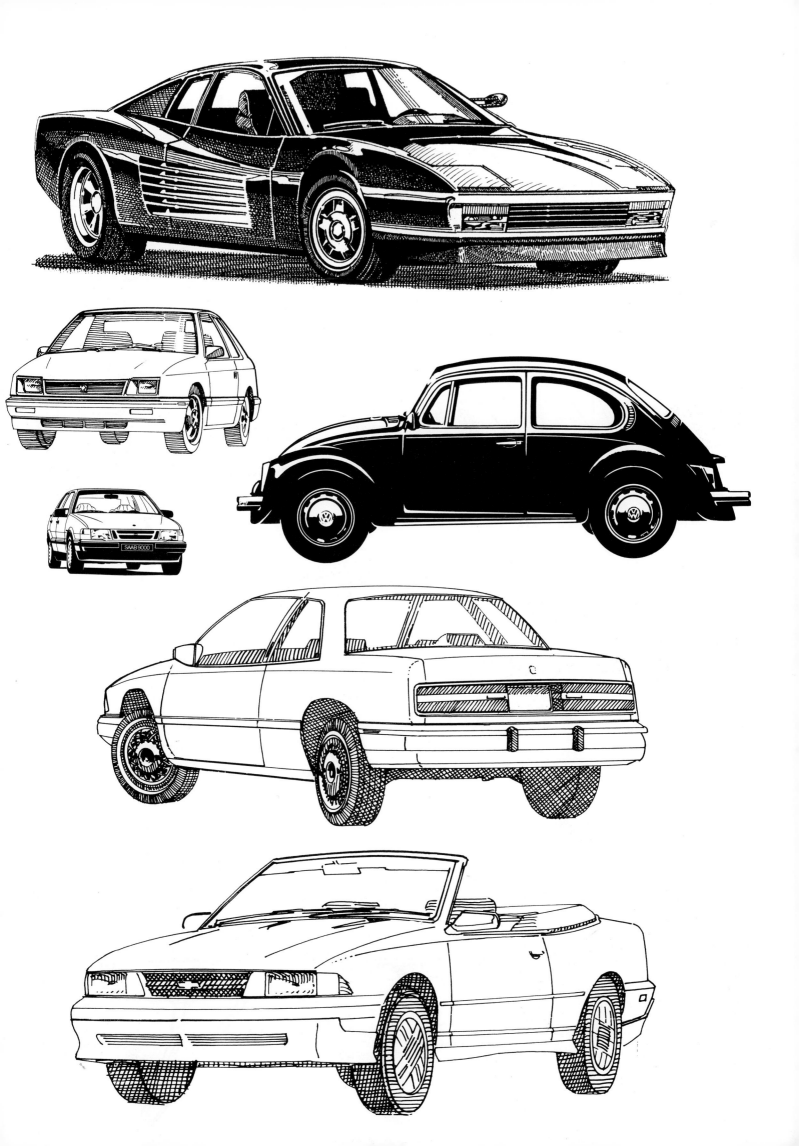

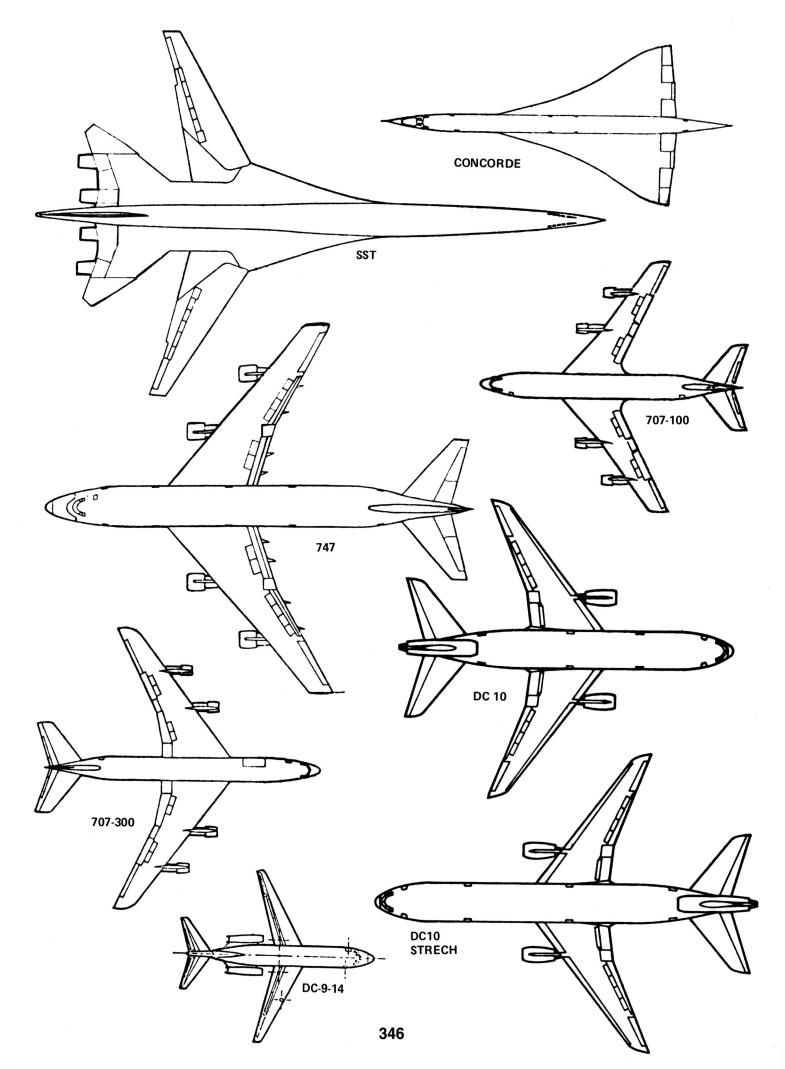

AIRPLANES   50 SCALE

CONCORDE

SST

707-100

747

DC 10

707-300

DC10
STRECH

DC-9-14

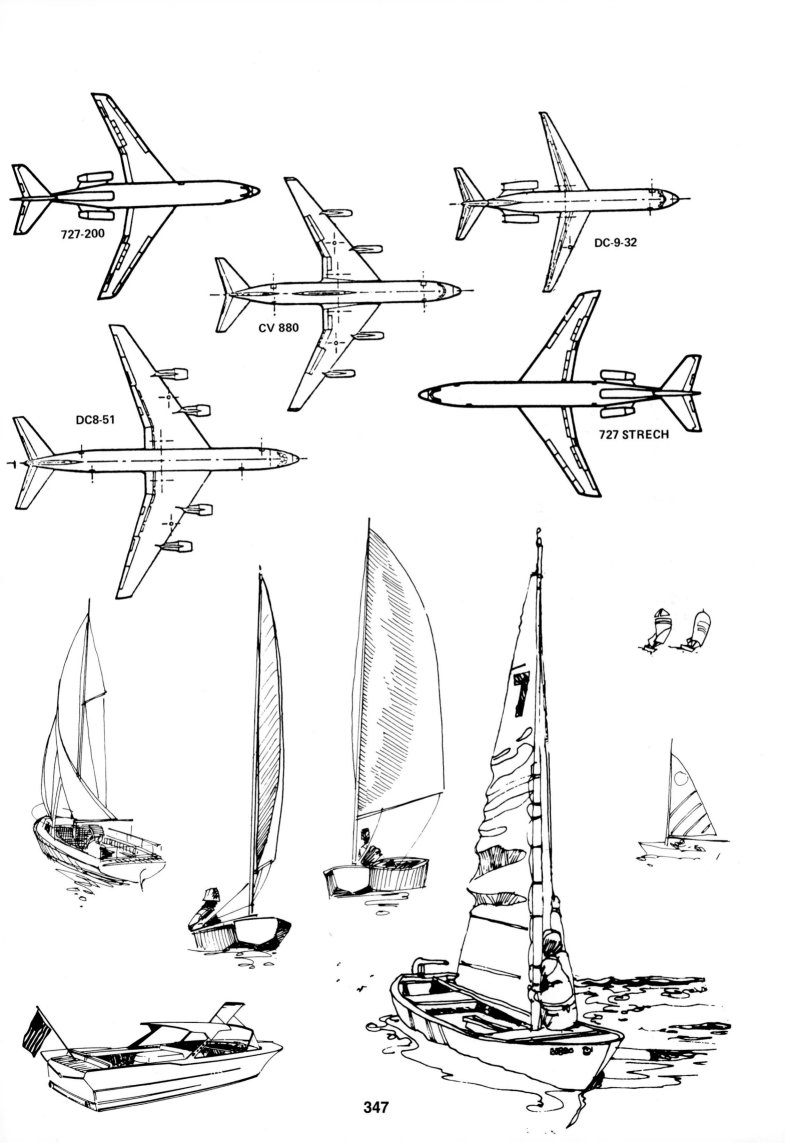

727-200

CV 880

DC-9-32

DC8-51

727 STRECH